BOUNDARIES

GRIEVING THE LIVING

DISCLAIMER:
The information provided in this book is intended for general informational and educational purposes only. While the author is a licensed mental health professional, this book does not constitute personalized medical or psychological advice, diagnosis, or treatment.

Readers should not use the content of this book as a substitute for professional judgment or as a replacement for individualized advice from a qualified mental health or medical professional. Always consult with a licensed professional for advice tailored to your specific circumstances.

Always seek the advice of a qualified health care provider with any questions you may have regarding a medical or psychological condition. Never disregard professional or mental health advice or delay seeking it because of something you have read in this book.

The use of this book does not establish a therapeutic or professional relationship between the reader and the author. The author disclaims any liability for actions taken or not taken based on the information presented in this book.

First Edition.

What If? Publishing:
Managing Editor: Robin Shukle
Design: Liz Mrofka

ISBN: 979-8-9914775-0-5

BOUNDARIES

GRIEVING THE LIVING

LAURA MOULTON, MA

ACKNOWLEDGMENTS

Thank you to my husband for putting up with my neuroticism as I wrote this book. You make me feel like I can do anything, and I am forever grateful of your support and making me feel like I am worth all the trouble I am. Thank you to my beautiful daughters who inspire me to write for the younger generation, so you and those you care about can be more emotionally healthy and know exactly how to deal with pain. Thank you to my amazing publishers who believed in me and helped me believe publishing this book was worth the fear and vulnerability. Thank you to my in-laws as they have been amazingly supportive through this journey and have expressed their pride in me as a daughter-in-law. Thank you to my sister, you showed up when you didn't have too. I have to thank my two cats for their judgmental looks and unfavorable companionship, they really did a great job telling my husband he is their favorite. Lastly, thank you to each of you that knew I was writing this book and encouraged me along the way. I am very blessed to have friends like you who felt that this message was worth sharing. Please enjoy!

AUTHOR'S NOTE

Writing this was a challenge for me. I am an introvert and I care very much about the healing of others. I am used to consistent feedback when I talk to someone, and writing a book doesn't provide that! I love to have a back story, read facial expressions, learn mannerisms, listen to language, empathize with emotions, reflect understanding, and provide clarity. Without that data it is hard to tailor my message to someone's individual needs. I appreciate knowing that what I am trying or attempting to say is getting absorbed by the receiving party. Therefore, please give me grace if something does not land well—that is not my intention. I do hope I am able to connect with you somehow, and you pick up on some of my playful sarcasm.

I wrote this book because I got frustrated if I am being honest. I kept having the same conversation over and over again. I kept seeing patterns that were heartbreaking. I noticed similar behaviors in people where they were changing how they think, how they believe, how they talk, and how they behave, just so they can save a relationship they think they need. People were willing to give away so much of themselves for the sake of keeping an unhealthy relationship. I knew there had to be a way to hold more people's hand through this pain. I didn't want anyone to feel like the pain will swallow them up. I wanted to give empowerment if I could. I wanted to do what I could to make sure you never had to live a life of self betrayal ever again. I know it was a fight worth having personally, I hope it is for you as well.

TABLE OF CONTENTS

PREFACE

I wrote this section specifically for those who identify as a Christian, and want to gently direct my attention towards you. We have the potential to, and have indeed caused, more harm to those in grief than many other groups. It is not our job to play God and decide who is making a good or bad decision about a tough relationship. If *asked* an opinion we may offer one. To make quick judgements, decisions, and offer unsolicited platitudes is unfair and can be received by others as spiritually abusive. One way to help stop this is to notice it is happening and deal with our own unhealed grief so we can be more present for others as they go through it. Regardless of the type of loss someone feels, the pain is still under the grief umbrella.

Our culture is riddled with phrases that appear to be helpful but are actually harmful to our emotional healing journey. Platitudes that are not helpful promote messages to people that are often dismissive, belittling, condescending, patronizing, and downright abusive. Since this is an itch I cannot avoid scratching as I talk about the emotional healing of others, I do address the spiritual abuse aspects of how Christians tend to unintentionally *promote avoidance* of grief and pain. Platitudes are rarely helpful. Giving people an idea of what *we believe* they need to hear in pain, rarely lands well with the receiver. If you are someone who feels better after someone says: "God doesn't give you more than you can handle," or "God hears your pain," or "I'll pray for you," or "We all go through this at some point," or "There are worse things in life," then don't listen to me. I have heard more times than not that these phrases and similar cause people to grieve longer than need be. These are ideally not the way to help. These phrases appear to cause a lot more damage than good. Listen to those in pain and show up empathetically, don't decide for them what they need to hear. Just hear them out. Acknowledge and reflect words *they* use and be vulnerable with them.

If you do not identify as someone who has a relationship with Jesus Christ or who feels any biblical obligations, you may skip the appendix or other areas as needed. This content is intended for those who may have overlooked the idea that we have a higher accountability for our behaviors. Whatever belief or God you ascribe to, the message is for those who believe they have a responsibility in this life and must answer for their choices. I am the first to admit that interpreting the Bible is not a strength of mine. Therefore, I give my best ideas and understandings in the appendix section. That is why I attempt to address our ability to hurt others, and how we allow others to hurt us.

For those who identify with the Christian faith or other higher power(s), it is up to us not to promote psychological harm to those who wish to better understand God and build healthy relationships. It is our job to encourage healing and healthy relationships not to stagnate or damage them; therefore, we will have to answer for every maltreatment we have done. That is a big deal. We must take our own healing, and other's emotional healing, seriously. We must be gentle but direct: not to be in the business of brutal honesty (unless needed) but rather in gentle honesty, caring honesty, and loving honesty. I hear this phrase a lot: "I didn't want to lie to them!" Sure, please don't lie to them, but the impact of your delivery can be spiritually abusive and fundamentally unhelpful and even more hurtful.

When it comes to our own healing as followers, truth makes us better. Truth allows for growth. Accountability means growth and healing. As we walk through this journey together in grief, your job is to engage with the uncomfortable or hard parts. If you avoid these parts, you will miss the entire point of this book. Loss means you are healing, you are trying, and what you are doing matters to you and those you love. Our pain easily gets translated to those around us. It is often a very subtle change of behavior to our eyes. Typically, other people can notice the change in us faster than we can ourselves. It is important to use a critical lens and be receptive to the message and really check with other people to see if spiritual abuse is a pattern.

This allows for growth. Growth starts with acknowledgment. Once we have that acknowledgment healing becomes a choice. I hope this clarification helps us learn where we are making mistakes as followers and directs us to more education on how we are designed—to encourage and be in relationships with one another when it comes to pain and loss.

INTRODUCTION

Boundaries: a very popular topic for those who are invested in their self-help journey. Many books are written about it by such authors as Cloud and Townsend, Brené Brown, and many more. The gap I believe most of them have left is how to navigate the grief involved in creating and maintaining boundaries and the benefit we obtain after processing that grief. Grieving the living is often a point of healing that is not addressed. This is just a fancy term for saying goodbye to someone who is still alive. For many of us, it is the grief of someone saying, "I do not choose you; I do not want you; I do not love you." If you have ever experienced a hard breakup, then you understand grieving the living. My hope is to dive deeper into your relationships and see where you may need some guidance on grieving. When we grieve, we obtain some perspective changes we may not have been able to see before. The information shifts to another part of our brain and we feel differently. Have you ever cried really hard about something? How did you feel after? How did your perspective shift on that topic? Did you ever return to the issue to re-grieve it? If you did, did it feel different than the first time you cried about it? The answers to these questions are often the most rewarding after grieving a loss. However, most people forget this easily—or they fear the pain of obtaining the answer to these questions. I hope to help make you less afraid of your grief. If you do, boundaries are one of the most freeing benefits of grieving done well. There are quite a few benefits, but feeling empowered in yourself and how you want to live your life is well worth the pain in my opinion. I hope to help guide you to that freedom.

It is difficult to find literature that discusses the emotional cost of maintaining boundaries. Most likely because it is uncomfortable and painful to explore. For most, creating and upholding your boundaries is scary. While establishing and maintaining healthy boundaries is undeniably valuable, it requires considerable self-awareness, knowledge, and discipline. Now remember, not all scary things are bad. They just *feel* bad. There is a difference between something feeling bad and being good for you and something feeling bad and being bad for you. Working out is a great example. If you understand weight training or running, you know how awful it feels to start up the process. It is only after you put in hard work that you see the benefit of such suffering. Emotional health is not all that different. A healthy relationship with your inner self, and with others, requires difficult work to begin. Let's start you off by helping you through these difficult ideas and processes to grow to your full emotional potential. A common fear I hear is, "I can't start crying about this because if I do, I will never stop!" This is never something I have seen before. Have you? Have you seen someone never stop crying? You were designed to handle hard emotions. Your body and brain are, quite literally, designed to heal themselves. A skinned knee or other bodily injury generally heals itself with or without your permission. Emotions, on the other hand, need your permission and active intent to heal, hurt, and grow more mature. This is scary—but what if it is worth it?

Let's define some words before we get started, just so we are on the same page. Worthiness has many definitions—so let's narrow it down. When we talk about worthiness, we will associate it with who you are as a "worthy person." A lot of people have a feeling about what it means but don't know how it is practiced. This can lead to unhealthy mentalities like entitlement, self-inflated egos, insecurity, self-image problems, and negative world views. As a foundation to any continuing healing, it is necessary to establish a baseline of what your beliefs in this field are. For the purposes of this book I will be using worthiness to mean *acting in such a way to be deserving of the rights and dignities bestowed on us.* I believe this to be a good working definition. As we go about establishing what being a worthy person means, I urge you to recognize that, well, **you are a person**. A person who is just being a person has worth! Therefore, we ask those around us to treat us as such.

Now, when I talk to people about this idea that they are each a person with worth, they don't deny it at first and usually give me a weird look. When we go into how this looks, people are surprised that they exclude themselves from being a person all the time! My favorite approach to this is something I call "people logic." If you would never treat a **person** badly, then you cannot excuse yourself from **being a person**. It sounds so silly, but so many of you believe that you get to excuse yourself from being a human. If someone **else** is a human, so are **you**. You can try to logic your way out of this, but good luck! You can't. I'm right. I did not write this book for any recently discovered aliens, so I assume that everyone reading this book is a person. You, however, must see yourself as such. You have to start at this stance before you can continue your healing journey. If you cannot see yourself as a person, you will consistently keep pushing yourself to being "sub" human or "super" human, in states where you feel that you will either never be enough no matter what you do or want or that you would need to have superpowers to be enough. At that point, you would just continue to lie to yourself, and we can't let that happen. You are a human whether you are okay with it or not. We must be cognitively and emotionally logical going forward. Now that you know that emotions follow a logical path, go back to the fact that you cannot see yourself as above or below human. Include yourself in the human category. Since you now include yourself in the human category, you cannot speak to yourself in a way that you wouldn't to another human. Keep that mantra in your head as we continue this: If you wouldn't say it to someone else, you cannot say it to yourself. To quote Donald Hebb, "Neurons that wire together fire together, neurons that wire apart fire apart. (Hebb, 1949) " If you start to notice that you are not talking to yourself like a human being, immediately make a statement in your head that corrects it to help undo that neuron connection.

Yes, there is such a thing as emotional logic. No, it is not counter-intuitive. They show up for us when we need to pay attention to something in our life. Emotions show up for a reason. The logic is to follow that reason to its rightful conclusion. You will know what that

resolution is once you hit it—*it feels like your mind and heart align.*
Here is an example of emotional logic: The bachelor dude who has
struggled finding a long-term romantic partner. He constantly finds
reasons why a girl isn't enough for him. She snores too loud, she talks
too much, she texts often, or myriad other problems. He proceeds to
ditch her to find a new girl. The pattern continues. Then one day you
sit down and chat with the bloke, and he states that he feels so lonely,
and drinking is his favorite thing to do in a day. He feels that no one
wants him and hates that he is lonely all the time. Rather than recognizing the root of his loneliness, he blames women. So in his mind
every girl is not good enough for him and that is women's fault, even
though he is the one pushing women away. Thats rich. He created his
own loneliness. Therefore, his emotion—lonely—is logically based
on the situation he created. Emotions all tie back to something that
makes sense. That is, they do **if** you understand what you are seeing. If
you are someone that believes that emotions don't play an important
role in your maturity and healing, you will want to argue with me.
It is important that every emotion you feel through this journey of

IT IS IMPORTANT THAT EVERY EMOTION YOU
FEEL THROUGH THIS JOURNEY OF LOSS IS VALIDATED
AS HAVING MERIT. YOU ARE NOT CREATING OR
"MAKING UP" EMOTIONS WHEN YOU ARE HURT.
IT IS OUR JOB TO FIGURE OUT HOW THE HURT
CONTINUES TO HURT US AND HEAL IT.
WE CANNOT BE OKAY STAYING THE VICTIM.
WE MUST WANT TO MOVE ONWARD.

loss is validated as having merit. You are not creating or "making up" emotions when you are hurt. It is our job to figure out how the hurt continues to hurt us and heal it. We cannot be okay staying the victim. We must want to move onward.

Next is emotional immaturity, which we will define as: *the belief that one is entitled to their emotional state and hands the responsibility of that feeling to others.* Emotionally immature people are not interested in why they feel the way they feel. They just care that they are right in their emotions and don't care to self-reflect on why that is a problem. We see a lot of this in our society. It is entitled for us to believe that our emotions, which have manifested without clear understanding, should be the responsibility of others. That is not how emotions are designed to be. Emotionally mature people, on the other hand, are very articulate in why they feel what they feel and do not weaponize their emotions to abuse others with them. It's a spectrum, you see. It is necessary to understand yourself and articulate your emotions for healthy conflict resolution; it is really a basic skill set for developing sustainable relationships. I mention this because I think those of us— me included—that really value logic sometimes try to discredit that healing involves emotions. We need to accept that healing is logical, therefore emotions have a sense of logic to them. Within the emotional maturity spectrum, you can have healthy, well-articulated emotions or unhealthy destructive emotions.

Hopefully we have come to an agreement concerning the meanings of the terms above: worthiness, people logic, emotional logic, emotional immaturity, and emotional maturity. If these sound like ideas you can get on board with, then we may go through this journey better understanding each other. While we are on the topic of understanding each other, let's start with your family of origin. That's a fancy term for your family in which you spent your childhood with. Our family of origin is often what gives us the road map on how to navigate relationships. We model after our parents because we kind of have to until we developmentally can make our own decisions. Some of us had wonderful maps to relationships thanks to our parents, and others of us had no maps or literally every single wrong thing on the map! For those of us who have had very few things right on our map, my examples often lean toward you. The reason my examples do this is because if you can read the worst-case scenario, you can more easily navigate the lesser scenarios. Therefore, know that the examples I give are for those who have had really bad maps or few good things in their maps because the grief in those journeys is often brutal.

I want to provide a better map for those who may have grown up in a family where you were told very clearly that you are not loved, desired, or important. You may have been told that you are an insignificant person in the world, and no one wants you. When you are raised to believe that love is conditional, beliefs about yourself can get rather dark. Conditional love is receiving love only after you have earned it in the eyes of the person granting the love. Self-worth is severely hindered when you **only** understand love as conditional. All healthy relationships do have conditions. That is another word for boundaries. However, healthy conditions and conditional love are very different. One breeds perfectionism to gain worth and love and the other stops emotional abuse. I hope to help you stop emotional, verbal, and spiritual abuse and not feel bad about it. To be unapologetically in love with the person you are and who you are becoming means you, and others, have boundaries.

~~~~~~~~~~~~~~~

We will get into different relationships and how each have their own grief when boundaries are put into place. Let's look at ways to define boundaries and grief. Brené Brown provides a popular definition of boundaries in her book *Atlas of the Heart* when she describes them as "what's okay and what's not okay." One example she uses is that ". . . it is okay to be inspired by her work, but not okay to copy it and sell it." Another is that, "It's okay to be pissed. It's not okay to raise your voice and pound on the table" (p. 130, *Atlas of the Heart*). Brown quotes Prentis Hemphill in expressing, "Boundaries are the distance at which I can love you and me simultaneously" (pg. 129, *Atlas of the Heart*). Her description of grief in *Atlas of the Heart* is, "Grief is often thought of as a process that includes many emotions, rather than a singular emotion. For a long time, we thought about the grief process in terms of linear stages, but almost all of the recent research actually refutes the idea that grief progresses in predictable sequenced stages" (p. 110). She goes on to quote Robert Niemeyer, who states, "A central process in grieving is the attempt to reaffirm or reconstruct a world of meaning that has been challenged by loss" (p. 110). For the purposes of this book, we are going to define boundaries as follows: *Boundaries are respecting the decisions that other people have already made about you.* It is asking those around you to be treated like a person with the rights, dignity, respect, and consideration of any other person. For the purposes of this book, we will also define grief like this: *Grief is the process of setting loose a piece of your soul and knowing you cannot return to it.* It is the process of saying goodbye to something/someone that was very precious to you or something/someone you identified with. This process often includes mixed emotions to help heal the wound loss has created.

The danger of not following your own boundaries is living a life of never feeling like you are worthy of being enough, to never demand that you have dreams that should be honored and respected, to never feel that you are deserving of even minimal affection. I don't know anyone who would choose to live like that. Having boundaries helps fulfill your life, not limit it. This journey is about finding people whom you feel fulfilled and loved by. It is a good thing that not everyone is your person. If everyone were our "people," then we would be sacrificing ourselves to have their love, and honestly not everyone is healthy, which makes this a dangerous trade. Be picky about your people, don't accept everyone, and know that not everyone is willing to heal the way you are, and that is okay. That doesn't make this process any less sad. Saying goodbye to people who will not show up for us or love us is devastating. We need to make sure we are saying goodbye in an emotionally healthy way. We can't let rejection make decisions for us in our life. So let's learn how to grieve the living, starting with boundaries.

CHAPTER ONE

THE IMPORTANCE OF STICKING TO BOUNDARIES

Boundaries allow for accountability. Accountability is becoming severely depleted in our society. Some people constantly assume a victim mentality and desire to blame others for their own bad decisions or lack of decisions. Accountability is a necessary component of trust. You need trust to build and hold a relationship. Let me tell you why boundaries are so necessary. Boundaries not only hold people accountable for their actions but also teach them how to treat you. I hope from our earlier discussion you are not okay with anyone treating you as less than a person. Because you are a person. Boundaries and distancing yourself appropriately allow people to lose someone as important as you in their life. It is a natural consequence for their bad choices. Sometimes this is necessary for people to heal. Some people need to exhaust all relationships and hit rock bottom before they are going to change their behavior. You keep saving them? You are the one paying the price for their choices over and over and over and then wondering why you are so exhausted? Huh! Weird . . . How did that happen? It is almost like your exhaustion has some emotional logic to it! Wild world we live in.

Saving people from their own choices is very, very dangerous. It teaches them that they can ruin other people's lives and never have to deal with the consequences. Look at our political authority figures now! They seem totally fine taking advantage of people because they have been able to manipulate intricate systems into never giving them consequences. That is not healthy. It also creates a dangerous and scary society because if poor choices don't have natural consequences, then everyone can hurt everyone else, and it is no one's fault! That creates a lack of safety, and when people feel unsafe, they will do scary things. This is why boundaries are necessary. Boundaries oftentimes means safety.

No one should ever in your life have a "pass" for hurting you continuously. That pass should not be "mother," "father," "husband," "wife," or "child." No one should be treated like they are not human.

One thing that is difficult to think about is: What do we do when the scary people we need boundaries with are our family members? We will dive more into this in a future chapter, but the logic that leads to making allowances—because it's your mom, it's your dad, it's your brother, sister, dog, whatever—those are not *reasons* to continue to be abused. It doesn't matter how someone is related to you. I will forever stand by my statement that just because someone is someone to you, it does not mean you should be continually beaten down and hurt by them. No one should ever in your life have a "pass" for hurting you continuously. That pass should not be "mother," "father," "husband," "wife," or "child." No one should be treated like they are not human. If you want to continue letting others treat you poorly, that is your decision! I won't ever tell someone what to do, but I will say that too many people give other people passes for the weirdest and most random reasons and then wonder why they are sad when, again, it is clearly obvious why they are sad.

Boundaries give people the consequences they need to change behavior, if they will ever change behavior. Now, this is very hard work. Hard. Like, really hard! Don't beat yourself up because boundaries, and the grief associated with them, take practice. Emotional resiliency is a skill set. All skills need a lot of practice to be good at them! The price for a while is typically feelings of loneliness and disappointment, but it is not because *you* chose it, it is because *they* chose it, and that's why boundaries are made. Boundaries mean we respect the decisions that other people have made *about us*. We must respect what other people have already chosen about us. That is very sad once you see clearly how they view you based on how they treat you, but you cannot continue to push someone else into seeing you in a way that they are unwilling to see you. Therefore, goodbyes are necessary.

It is possible that boundaries are not forever, but if someone continues to treat you like you are not a person and are unworthy of affection, attention, or communication, you **must** respect that! They won't change if you are closer to perfect, better, smarter, or gain more accolades. None of that will matter because they have already made a decision about you. The goal is learning how to respect other people's boundaries, which are decisions they have already made about you, and then healing from other people's decisions. Later, we will look at what it feels like to be on the other side of a goodbye. The next section goes into the benefit of having grieved through something well. Emotional processing is a term I use for better understanding a situation and being able to absorb that messaging. When we Emotional process something painful is a lot like Phoenix mythology: In death there is life.

One of the saddest things we reconcile with when it comes to boundaries is that we cannot ever have the power to change the people we love. We cannot ever make someone love us, we cannot make someone see us as worthy, and we cannot make someone see us as important. That is not possible. We grieve that reality and say goodbye to the power over others that we never had. In the next chapters, we will look at the types of relationships in which we must grieve and say goodbye to them, or part of them, if we are to instill boundaries to protect ourselves from being treated as subhuman. Each relationship has a unique type of grief that we will address. Every person's grief is different, but what is most important is learning how to honor your emotional needs and not betray yourself.

Remember that boundaries are on a spectrum based on your needs—therefore so is grief. We will look at different relationships and how to navigate some drastic examples. Losing the entire relationship is often the biggest fear. On the lightest end of the spectrum, boundaries often sound like, "I will just not discuss this topic with this person." There is grief involved in that, of course, it is just a milder form of loss for a particular topic. That grief looks and feels very similar and has a familiar sting. However, the map I will provide in this book is to guide you through possible worst cases. With that map, you can navigate other situations accordingly.

*SEE APPENDIX FOR A POTENTIAL SPIRITUAL ABUSE PITFALL FOR THIS SECTION.

CHAPTER TWO

ROMANTIC PARTNER

H ave you broken up with someone or had someone break up with you while dating? Then you understand the grief in grieving the living. When you break up with someone, it is typically because they have crossed a boundary with you or you with them. It is your responsibility to clearly mark those boundaries early in the relationship. The dangerous and overly "gamified" way dating is set up in today's world does not encourage hard conversations. Many people use the rationalization that you first need to make sure you click and "have fun" with someone on a first date. I wholeheartedly disagree with this. *Fun is a side effect of safety*. You cannot have fun without first establishing safety. For example, on a roller coaster, you get clicked into your seat. I don't know about the rest of you, but I double-check it when the person clicks me in. I must, in all situations, make sure I am completely safe in that seat before I can enjoy the ride. After I am safe, I know I can enjoy myself and get an adrenaline rush. Trying to have fun before safety is the same as getting on a roller coaster without your seat belt. It is reckless, careless, and results in unnecessary pain, all because you didn't find it important to make sure you were safe first. There are numerous examples of this, but the roller coaster really makes clear the feeling of being smashed onto your face because of irresponsibility on your end. If you do not see how this game is dangerous, then you will just continue to hurt yourself and blame everyone you are dating because you are not guarding your own heart and needs.

Now that we have cleared this up, I strongly recommend that you should treat dating like an interview. My husband and I agree that an interrogation is even better. This may sound intimidating or uncomfortable, but it is a very important step in establishing healthy boundaries. You tell me—do you want to break up after six months and grieve all that wasted time? Or barely start the relationship and not have to grieve at all? Your choice. This will be hard and uncomfortable. The question is do you want the hard and uncomfortable now or later?

IT IS YOUR JOB TO MAKE SURE THAT A PERSON YOU ARE INTERESTED IN BUILDING A LONG-LASTING RELATIONSHIP WITH SHARES YOUR VALUES, MORALS, NEEDS, DESIRES, DESIGN IN LIFE, POLITICS, RELIGION, KIDS, ETC. THAT STUFF NEEDS TO BE ADDRESSED WITHIN THE FIRST SEVERAL DATES AND OTHER SUBSEQUENT DATES IF IT IS NOT ALL ADDRESSED.

It really is that simple. Pick your uncomfortable. I encourage you to pick the hard conversations—the trade-off is a lot more painful, and all that pain is avoidable. It is your job to make sure that a person you are interested in building a long-lasting relationship with shares your values, morals, needs, desires, design in life, politics, religion, kids, etc. That stuff needs to be addressed within the first several dates and other subsequent dates if it is not **all** addressed. This is how you can establish emotional safety before you start enjoying the relationship.

What if you get all these questions out of the way early and this person is amazing? What if they align with you on all these things? You have immediate security in your relationship because you both have established and made agreements for the rest of the relationship on the basis of what you both desire. You are not having anxiety, you are not questioning motives, you are not wondering if you made them mad, you already have agreements on conflict resolution, and nothing but honest authenticity is now driving your relationship. Of course you need to make sure the other person holds true to their word throughout the relationship, but you will have boundaries already established to return too for clarification or augmentation of future goals.

Why on earth do so many people not want this? That is something I will never understand. I hope that the firm establishment of boundaries scares the wrong people away. The wrong people won't want to answer hard questions because they are not emotionally mature enough to handle a full-fledged relationship. Please pick emotionally mature people. It is necessary for relationship sustainability. The boundaries must be first out the gate. The wrong people will hate it, and the right people will love it. I often use this example with people: What if you are on a first date and you sit down at the table and say, "Thank you so much for meeting me today. I'm really glad we were able to do this, and I think it is important that I get some things out of the way first so you know what you would be getting into with me. First, I have been married before, and I do not have kids. It ended because I wanted kids and they didn't. I want to date someone who wants kids someday. Also, I was raised by a single mom, I do not have a father figure at all in my life, and it needs to be okay with you that you will never have a father-in-law and the kids won't have a (maternal/paternal) grandpa. I struggle with conflict resolution, and I am working on it. Historically, when I have stated my needs, the people in my life have been dismissive and told me I am wrong. I often need some encouragement if you notice me distancing myself because I don't like to upset people I care about. So far, is there any of that you are not okay with?"

Would you hate this or love this? People I have given this example, or similar, have said almost unanimously, "Wow that is really refreshing. I don't know if anyone is actually like that, though!" Newsflash: Everyone is capable of this. You just have to decide to do it. Now, think about how you would respond if you were **not** okay with something they say on the first couple of dates? For example, if someone says that their political party is this and not that, or their parenting style is this or not that, then you know right away. You can end a relationship with minimal or no emotional attachment versus waiting six months or more to figure out these key topics. This protects your heart and establishes safety right away. Then you can see if it is easier to have fun with someone when the hard questions are answered. I will never tell you what to do with your dating life, but if you are asking the questions, "Well, how do I date better?" or "How come I keep picking the same type of person?" or "Why do my relationships always fail at a certain time frame?" then, in my opinion, the best way to go about not running into the same problems with similar types of people is to set boundaries.

Now let's assume you got all the hard questions out of the way and you guys are in agreement on what constitutes a healthy relationship. So far, you have felt things are going very well! Then they decide to do something that completely ruins your trust. Pick the issue: cheating, lying to you, financially abusing you, keeping secrets, watching pornography, stealing, or another deal-breaker. This clearly has broken your original agreement, and you are devastated, presumably. This will often cause a flight/fight/freeze/fawn[1] response and make you spiral into what the next steps are. This is a terrifying moment for most people because it causes life-altering decisions.

I am going to say the thing you are not supposed to say: If you stay with this person after they have breached big or multiple boundaries, then you are giving them permission to continue to hurt you. You are saying with your actions, "You are allowed to treat me as subhuman

---

[1]Flight is when you run away from danger. Fight is when you fight off a dangerous situation. Freeze is when your body and mind stop moving to avoid danger. Fawn is when you will do the demands of others to make the danger stop or go away. (Walker, n.d.)

because I am unworthy of being treated like a person, and you clearly agree, therefore I am okay getting abused by you continually because that is all I am worthy of." That is horrible. You are complicit with someone who views you as someone who is worth betraying. It is your job to make sure no one ever gets permission to treat you like that. You wouldn't do it to them! Why is it okay that they do it to you? It's not—don't let it be.

Let's touch on the milder spectrum in a romantic relationship for when your partner breaches trust with you but it is not breakup or divorce worthy. If you do not tell your significant other that they have hurt you, then you will harbor resentment. Resentment is in the anger spectrum of emotion and has grief aspects attached to it. Resentment builds and builds until often an emotional blowup happens. It is unfair to blow up at someone when you have not discussed with that person what they did to you. If you have told them what they have done to hurt you and are noticing only minimal change or change for a limited amount of time, then that will corrode your relationship slowly if you don't make a boundary. For example, let's say you are constantly the person doing house chores and feel really exhausted because the division of labor is not equal in the house. You bring this up to your person, and they help more for one week but after that go right back to not helping anymore. You now have to make a decision about what this means for you. Does it mean you hire a maid for yourself? Does it mean laundry doesn't get done for the next 3 days? Does it mean dinner isn't made at all? It is not possible to handle all the labor of the house on your own. It's too hard. Therefore, something suffers. Not because something is wrong with you but because you are not superhuman and you cannot go beyond your capabilities. That is a boundary you have to decide on.

In large breaches of boundaries I strongly believe that if you don't let people have the consequence of losing you for their actions then they will never hit the bottom they need, and ruin the relationships they need, to establish change for themselves. Now, I feel if someone has betrayed you, it is necessary that you cut them off completely until they have gone through the right avenues to **earn** your trust back. Not be gifted your trust back—to earn it. If they *actually* care about you, they will work their tail off to gain trust back. It should take a lot of effort on their part because they were the ones who were okay hurting you for the sake of their own benefit. Forever punishment is not the answer either if you have decided to let them earn your trust back. There has to be a measurable point of at which you know you can trust them again.

Remember that forgiveness does not mean absolution, forgiveness just means you take your hand off their throat for what they have done (Young, 2008). Forgiveness is up to *you* not up to the betraying party to demand forgiveness from you. It is an abuse of power if the other party tries to make that argument. The person who hurt you does

FORGIVENESS IS UP TO YOU NOT UP TO THE BETRAYING PARTY TO DEMAND FORGIVENESS FROM YOU.

not get to decide whether forgiveness or absolution is their "reward" for treating you terribly. It is something you decide internally. Your behavior will show whether you have forgiven them or not, because you do or don't want to metaphorically take your hand off their throat.

If you have made it to this point without closing this book because I am offensive, that is awesome. Now we can get to the grief part. Going into the worst-case scenario: If you have broken up with a person, I strongly recommend you cut things off on all levels during a breakup. This is recommended because healing is necessary. It is kind of like if you had shards of a bullet in you. You cannot fully heal if shrapnel is still stuck in your skin. It all has to come out in order for things to heal. Start with your basics like Snapchat, Instagram, text, phone calls, WhatsApp, and perhaps even pictures depending on the situation. Cut them out completely. Grief will take much longer if you decide to keep one little shard left in you.

A lot of people argue with me here and say, "But what if we want to be friends?" That is cute, nice try, but when you get betrayed, friendship is not your first go-to, I hope. Also, anyone who tries to be friends with an ex is statistically ridiculously likely to wind up in a friends-with-benefits situation. That will ultimately make grief last longer and hurt your own feelings again. So, I am going to start with the assumption you are not betraying yourself and you have allowed yourself to heal from this betrayal. Friendship can come after complete healing. Some people need years and some need months. Trust yourself—don't betray yourself.

Now, Kübler-Ross lays out the 5 stages of grief: Denial, Bargaining, Sadness, Anger, Acceptance (2005). She is on record stating that grief does not go in a predictable order.[2] The rule when it comes to grief is that all emotions are valid. However, if you experience homicidal or suicidal responses, you need a higher level of care[3]. Just about everything else emotionally in grief is considered normal.

Let's talk about the normalcy of grieving a breakup. It is devastating to establish a boundary that means you can no longer live your life with someone with whom you have lived a portion of it. To choose that you are worth loving well because someone else won't is one of the loneliest and saddest journeys. Grief is a necessary emotion to being human. Learn to grieve well and you will not have to gaslight yourself into thinking something is wrong with you when you experience organic and healthy human emotions. Our macro society does that to us. It makes us believe we are crazy if we are sadder longer than 24 hours over something. That is so stupid. Emotion does what it does, and anyone who is grieving knows that it is a journey and a process, not something you just cry about and move on. Different things will

---

[4]If you are interested in Kübler-Ross's 5 stages, I would recommend the many books she has written to better dive into these: *On Death & Dying, On Grief & Grieving, On Life After Death, Life Lessons: Two Experts on Death,* and more. I will say for the purposes of this book that I am here to help validate the irreparable pain betrayal can create.

---

[3]If you are having homicidal or suicidal thinking please reach out to a hotline such as Suicide and Crisis Lifeline 988, or National Suicide Prevention Lifeline at 1-800-273-8255 if you are in the United States.

pop up, and you will need to grieve all the different pieces that break your heart. That is natural and healthy. If you do not grieve well, you will, *you will*, bring that into your next relationship because you are refusing to heal your issues. That brings us back to emotional maturity. Emotionally mature people continually work hard to heal all aspects that continue to hurt them in their day-to-day lives. It is an ongoing process. When it comes to emotions, it is not one and done.

Give yourself all the permission and time you need to cry. Let yourself feel the pain. I often recommend a good playlist. Mine is currently named "Have a Festive Mental Break Down." It is honestly a wonderful playlist when I need it. Really gets the waterworks going. Find a safe space to cry. I would encourage you to only cry around safe people—those that won't hold it against you—otherwise, do it alone. Let it happen for as long as it needs to happen. Favorite places for people often include the shower, clothes closet, car, garage, or bathtub. Let yourself feel what you need to feel and know that it *does* have an end. We can be grateful for this because our emotions have something called hedonic adaptation by Philip Brickman and Donald Campbell in "Hedonic Relativism and Planning the Good Society (1971)." It is a fancy term that ". . . refers to the notion that after positive or negative events (i.e., something good or bad happening to someone), and a subsequent increase in positive or negative feelings, people return to a relatively stable baseline level of affect" (Diener, Lucas, & Scollon, 2006, Science Direct). Do you remember the first time your significant other said I love you? Can you remember the feeling you got when you heard it? That feeling dulled down after awhile right? Now you say I love you and don't get the same intense and powerful feelings. When you grieve a relationship the power and intensity of those first "I love you" feelings have to be broken apart. It is why the first moment of you realizing the relationship is over is so devastating. It is the undoing of all the amazing and powerful emotions that came before. The first initial emotional responses are so powerful due to hedonic adaptation.

This is important to keep in mind when you are attempting to avoid crying. Grief *does* have a far side. Hedonic adaptation kicks in because our brains are wired for it. However, the data is moving from where the grief is to another part of the brain, which is exhausting neurologically. That's why most people are tired after they cry. Remember, crying ends for a time—and comes back in the waves it needs—to be able to file data well in your brain's system.

IT IS NECESSARY TO SEE THE IMPORTANCE OF GRIEVING THE BOUNDARY OF AN ENDED SIGNIFICANT-OTHER RELATIONSHIP. THERE IS A TON OF GRIEF WHEN WE CEMENT OUR STANCE ON NOT ALLOWING PEOPLE TO HURT US CONTINUALLY.

It is necessary to see the importance of grieving the boundary of an ended significant-other relationship. There is a ton of grief when we cement our stance on not allowing people to hurt us continually. We no longer let them prove to us that we are unlovable, unworthy humans. This means addressing the ways in which their actions and attitudes impact our self-worth and destroy our dreams and best images of ourselves. Setting a boundary requires many necessary pieces to heal the grief of a relationship. Saying goodbye to someone who betrays your trust, hurts you, and lies to you in a romantic situation will always be heartbreaking, but sacrificing yourself so someone can continually hurt you has no logical basis and will create a self-sabotaging cycle. You are too important to let someone else decide your future. Heal well—be there for those who need you in your future.

Katie and Tim have been together for a year and a half. Katie noticed one day that she never asked her boyfriend what his definition of flirting was. It came to her one day because she was out having lunch with her best friend Joann at work and a guy came up and asked for Joann's number. Joann was batting her eyes, laughing a bit more than normal, and said that he could follow her on Snapchat. Then the guy takes his leave. Katie asks Joann why she would give that guy any information when she knows she has a boyfriend. Joann said that her and her boyfriend agreed that anyone is allowed to follow them on their Snapchat story but no where else, and they have limited to no conversation with anyone who seems interested in them. Katie had never thought about this before and it made her wonder if she was okay with Tim doing something like this. She goes home that night to start up the conversation. She asks, "If you were to define flirting what would you say that is?" Tim gets a scared look on his face and says, "What do you mean?" Katie says, "I never considered asking what flirting was to you because we seemed so sure on our relationship." Tim retorts with, "Then why are you asking now?" Katie starts to feel more suspicious because he is not answering the question. She says, "Just answer the question!" Tim says, "I mean, I have a work wife. I never told you about it because it was harmless and it didn't mean anything. I think some people would think that is flirting. I don't though." Katie starts to get uncomfortable. "What do you mean a work wife? Who is it and why is she called that?" Tim starts to think about how he defines flirting and is wondering if she is going to be mad about this.

What do you think Katie and Tim did right in this conversation? What boundaries may have been misunderstood? What do you think they can do to make boundaries together around this topic? Do you see where this problem could have gotten out of hand?

*SEE APPENDIX FOR A POTENTIAL SPIRITUAL ABUSE PITFALL FOR THIS SECTION.

CHAPTER THREE

PARENTS

~~~~~~

This section has an exceptional sting to it. If you have a wonderful relationship with both of your parents, you are a very lucky person. A good majority of people tend to mostly like their parents. Another group tends to sometimes or somewhat like their parents. The last group of people will never feel safe with or even like their parents.

Each one of these dynamics require boundaries. Our parents are very special and delicate relationships in our lives. Our parents are the people who can hurt us the most and encourage us the fastest. They make us feel very seen and loved or can destroy our sense of self in a matter of a couple sentences. Being a parent is a very powerful position to be in. As we become adults, we have the ability to stand up for ourselves and set boundaries we were not able to as kids. This becomes tricky as each child reaches adulthood. These boundaries will change once you move out and get your own place, get married, have children, or get a dog. Each stage provides for a different set of rules, boundaries, and behaviors.

It is amazing to me when I ask people what their relationship is like with their parents. Almost everyone I see will say, "Oh, I had a great childhood!" or "I really like my parents" or "I have nothing but good things to say!" I then ask, "Oh, that's great! Like how? Or why?" The majority of people instantly get a stunned and confused look on their face. They will often say, "Well, I don't know. I guess they were there for me and stuff." I will say, "Oh, like how?" At this point I encounter strong defensiveness, such as, "What do you mean like how! Like how a parent is there for you!" Which I have to retort with, "Okay great, can you give me an example where you really felt that?" Then they stay mad at me for a while. The other option they say is, "Oh, umm, well, maybe this (one or two events)." I then ask, "Okay, anything you wish would be different?" This is where I get the very long stories of how they have been hurt by their parents and feel like what they are asking for really isn't all that hard, but one or more of their parents make them feel like it is impossible. So often, they immediately start gaslighting themselves and state things like, "Well, I ask for too much" or "I think I expect her to do more than she does" or "I think she's/he's just done enough already, you know?"

What is so sad about this is that a lot of things children are asking of their parents are realistic and often very human asks: simple things. For example, a popular one is an apology. "I wish my mom would apologize to me for that instance in high school when she commented on how big I looked in the dress I was trying on for prom" or "I wish my dad would apologize for not standing up for me when I needed him to against mom" or "I just wish my mom would apologize for being so critical of me all the time!" Other examples are acknowledging my emotions and expressing that they care about me, think I am important, and want to tell me how proud of me they are. It is devastating when we realize that our parents won't do this not because they **cannot** but because they **will not**. Parents often believe they are "above" telling their children something they think they should already know or apologize for something they aren't sorry for. This literally destroys the souls of your children. I don't know a single person, even if they are eighty years old, who doesn't want to feel loved, seen, heard, accepted, appreciated, and wanted by their parents.

I know that it is very rare for a child to not have tried every single avenue they could possibly think of to get their parents to love them. These attention-seeking behaviors include things like perfectionism, addiction, social isolation, accolades, popularity, pursuit of beauty, people pleasing, over-responsibility, and confrontation. It is very unlikely that if you just try this one phrase or one behavior, then BAM—your mom and/or dad will love you! That is just not the case. You have probably tried *every* possible thing you could think of to restore or create a healthier relationship with your parent(s). If you feel you have not tried every avenue—"Because I know my mom and if I did that then [fill in consequence here]"—at some point you learned that behavior isn't desirable. For example, maybe you didn't try perfectionism because you knew it would be a threat to your mom's ego. Remember, the age you are is how long you have known your parents. Therefore, you have that many years of data. That's a lot of time to prove yourself right!

I DON'T KNOW A SINGLE PERSON, EVEN IF THEY ARE EIGHTY YEARS OLD, WHO DOESN'T WANT TO FEEL LOVED, SEEN, HEARD, ACCEPTED, APPRECIATED, AND WANTED BY THEIR PARENTS.

Sometimes parents want to try, and they engage when you talk to them about what hurts you. One of the best feelings in the world is when you say what hurt you and what you need from them, and they say, "Sweetie, I am so sorry. That was really unfair of me to do that to you. You mean the world to me. I would never want to hurt your feelings and make you feel the way I did. I care too much about our relationship for you to ever feel belittled by me. I am sorry. I love you. I will work on this." And mean it! This is one of the most meaningful things you could possibly say to a child. If you ask any adult who has an unhealthy relationship with their parent, they will tell you that an affirmation like that would have completely changed their life. Those of you who do not have self-aware parents and in your head are thinking, "Yeah right! My mom/dad would never say that to me! [insert large eye roll here]" you are who I am talking to! Some of you read that line and started to tear up. How meaningful would that be? "Wow, I can't even imagine my mom/dad saying that. It really hurts that they wouldn't!"

So, I'm going to punch you in the gut here. Sadly, this isn't extraordinary. This isn't really even that hard. You're just asking to be seen as someone worthy of loving well. If someone chooses to not treat you—at this basic level—like a human, it doesn't matter if their title is "mom" or "dad." It is very possible that the person(s) who were your guardians don't see you as someone worthy of being treated like a person! This happens to people. For those this has happened to—I promise you are not alone.

It is important to clarify here that it is very difficult to decide which relationships require a few boundaries and which you need to cut off. No one, I mean no one, can ever make that decision for you. You are the only person who knows what you are okay with tolerating and what you are not okay with tolerating. You may hear thoughts, recommendations, or advice, but it *has* to sit well with you and you alone. That is why figuring out how many boundaries you need is up to you. You have a lot of options. Arguably, the most important thing to know about boundary-setting is that it is reasonable to request to be treated like a human by someone else. Boundaries only cause problems with unhealthy people. Healthy people handle boundaries just fine and tend to apologize and understand. An example of a reasonable request is, "I can't have you criticize my body when I come over for Thanksgiving. It is really hurtful, and I don't want to talk about it this year. Can we do that?" Any healthy person would easily comply with this. For a healthy person, this is a signal to them that you have been emotionally unsafe and wish to feel safe at this Thanksgiving event.

Unresolved grief has a way of popping up in our life in surprising ways. Let me show you how. When we think of something—some stimuli—our brain is wired to support that thought with memories of why we should feel the way we feel. Let's do an easy exercise. If I say the word "roller coaster," what is the first emotion that pops into your head? If it is "fun," then you probably have a memory of riding a favorite roller coaster and it being fun (memory to support the emotion). If that word is "scary," you probably are seeing an image of your head of a roller coaster gone wrong! Our brain is wired to support our emotions with memories to back them up. This is how grief follows us into our present day. When someone says a certain word to you—or makes you feel a certain way—all those memories pop up for why it was hurtful. This tends to show up in all our relationships one way or another. Think about when someone makes you feel really important, valued, and appreciated—I am sure you have an instance in your head when you felt that way. Now think of a time when you felt betrayed, confused, and belittled. Did you have a memory for any of those? These basic emotions **do** show up in relationships, even with our pets.

Let's look at another example. Let's say your mom is chatting with you about how you are parenting your kids. She has a strong opinion about why you are wrong about what you are doing. This is clearly upsetting to you, and this is one of the first times you decide to say something to your mom because she seems fine with critiquing you unfairly. You say something along the lines of, "Mom, I understand that is what you did with me, but that hurt me a lot growing up, and I will not continue that pattern." Let's say your mom gets super mad at you for saying this. She calls you ungrateful, says you hate her, that you have never appreciated all she has done for you, and that she finds you to be an entitled brat for confronting her like that. This type of situation is very common among new parents. What you may not be seeing in this situation is that your mom's reaction to you was defensive.

At this point the excuses and rationale tend to come out. Common questions and thoughts for processing of such aggressive and coldhearted behavior are often things like: What if your mom was never able to challenge her mom? What if your mom got reprimanded for even thinking something against her mom? What if your mom critiques you as hard as she critiques herself, which she learned from her mom? That issue is between your mom and grandma. Not you and your mom. But because your mom never healed that relationship, she is projecting those issues onto you. That is how grief is translated.

It will happen to you, too, in your next familial relationship if you do not heal the grief you need to. Grief is transferable. The sad part about grief is that it is transferable to children and spouses. Children get the brunt, and spouses get to witness it or be subjected to it.

Handling grief with parents is kind of a different animal in the sense that the repeated grief you face can often feel never-ending. Because parents are the ones that, you know, gave birth to us, we are nurtured with all the mannerisms, relationship models, morals, faith, religion, and other values that they showed us. Therefore, we have an ingrained sense of self that was developed by and learned from our

RESPECTING THE DECISIONS OUR PARENTS HAVE ALREADY MADE ABOUT US IS THE HEALTHIEST THING WE CAN DO FOR THEM, AND FOR OURSELVES, EVEN IF IT IS INCREDIBLY PAINFUL.

parents. Who we are and how we relate to the world—that has to get reworked. This is heavy stuff. It should, and often does, cause emotional exhaustion. That is a sign you are doing this right. It is helping you in your grief resiliency, if you will. This is the part where people often feel they will get lost in their sadness forever. I've never seen that happen, but it does feel that way. This is important to repeat because the brain likes to avoid pain—even if it is needed pain. As I've said previously, it should **feel** like you will drown in sadness, with a cognitive understanding that you will not literally do so. Respecting the decisions our parents have already made about us is the healthiest thing we can do for them, and for ourselves, even if it is incredibly painful. We can respect if they don't want a deep relationship with us or that maybe they don't want to feel as close as we need them to be or that they might not want to help us when we feel we need it. Whatever their boundary is, we cannot make them love us to the degree we may feel we want them to.

If this area is of particular interest to you—looking at the relationship you have with your parents—I would strongly recommend Lindsay Gibson's book *Adult Children of Emotionally Immature Parents.* She gives a great outline of definitions, has quizzes, and looks at potential pitfalls when handling parents. My particular favorite section of hers is "Being Cautious About New Openness." I agree with her statement, "But your job is to keep your adult outlook and continue relating to them [parents] as a separate, independent adult. At this point, you're looking for an adult relationship with them, not a re-creation of parent–child dynamics, right?" (pg. 156) She goes on to validate similar sentiments and states, "Just because a person is your biological parent doesn't mean you have to keep an emotional or social tie to that person" (pg. 165). If this relates strongly to you, coming to this realization about parents is heartbreaking.

Leslie is a new mom to her son Reid. Reid is only 2 years old. He is a very rambunctious little man and does enjoy playing rough. Leslie has to work today and really needs her mom's help watching him for about 4 hours today. Leslie's mom knows the schedule: Reid gets lunch, rides his bike for an hour, takes a nap, has a snack, and gets 30 minutes of TV time. Leslie drops Reid off with her mom and heads to work. When Leslie comes back to grab Reid, Leslie's mom has some updates to give her on Reid's day. Leslie's mom reports that he was throwing his food at lunch, played nice on the bike for the most part, fought his nap and laid down for about 30 minutes at best, and then only wanted to watch something Leslie's mom felt was very inappropriate so they had to turn off the TV. Leslie understood and it seemed like it all made sense. Then her mom says, "Leslie, I have no idea why you let your son act the way he does. He is so disrespectful and clearly you do not discipline him enough. He knows better at my house, and everything with him became a fight! You know how to parent better than this Leslie, I raised you better!" Leslie states, "Yes mom, you tell me this every week, I know you don't like the way I discipline Reid but I have tried to explain to you that the way you disciplined me is not how I want to discipline my son. I believe in a different model than you do." Leslie's mom bites back with, "Well it is wrong, and he needs to be more disciplined!" Leslie is exhausted from work and just wants to get home at this point. She thanks her mom for her help and goes back home. Leslie is talking to her husband later in the evening and says, "I cannot stand my mom getting mad about how we decided to discipline Reid! I mean who does she think she is? She doesn't even ask me what I am doing for discipline she just decides I am not doing a good job! Ugh, I am so frustrated because I need her help but I cannot stand how she talks to me after she watches him. I don't know what to do."

What are some ways Leslie might have a conversation with her mom? Do you think Leslie is stuck? If so, how come?

*SEE APPENDIX FOR A POTENTIAL SPIRITUAL ABUSE PITFALL FOR THIS SECTION.

42

CHAPTER FOUR

CHILDREN

~~~~~~

Our children are sometimes our most challenging relationships to hold onto when it comes to setting boundaries. I think what makes children more difficult to set healthy boundaries with is that they are a mirror and reflection of us. Everything our children learn to do, they watched us do first. Children look to us in their younger years to be their everything and as they get older, they look to us to support their everything even if it is unhealthy or scary. Children are a major component for a lot of people to have a very fulfilling life. The problem is, as parents, we have disappointment in our children when they do things that hurt their lives and those around them, and especially when they don't seem to have remorse. That is a very scary behavior to watch happen to our kids. They grow up and test boundaries and suck the life out of us, which I was told why most of us get gray hair. Children desperately need and desire boundaries. To them it means safety. I know you know that your mom cared when she got upset with you for running into the street after that ball. I know you know your dad cared when he got upset with you during your driving lesson and you jumped the curb. When our parents get upset with us and set boundaries, we know it is because they love us and want us to be safe. Ideally, our parents want us to be better people than they are! This is often very meaningful to us as adults.

If you are a parent, boundaries are necessary for expressing that you care about your child's safety and that they mean something to you. Some things, they will have to figure out the hard way, but that needs to be their decision, not yours. Lack of boundaries implies that you are fine if they are reckless. You are fine if they figure everything out the hard way. You are fine if they get hurt over and over again. Who needs guidance, anyway? Boundaries communicate love. We don't have to like that reality, but it is a fundamental component of love. Boundaries mean we know how to love well and love hard, the way that children need to thrive in their lives. Often, parents with no boundaries set their children up for a life of surviving and not thriving because everything is chaotic, confusing, dysregulating, lonely, and

PARENTS HAVE MORE SAY IN THE DESIGN OF THEIR CHILD'S LIFE THAN THEY COULD POSSIBLY IMAGINE.

sad. Again, we are using the definition of being treated like a person for boundaries. So, yes, these are the direct symptoms of not being treated like a person. Parents have more say in the design of their child's life than they could possibly imagine. Your child as an adult will either look at the world as a place to grow, experience, adventure, and try or as a devastating reality they are forced to survive. That worldview is put there by you as the parent. This is all I will say about the parents' role in raising children because there are many books on healthy boundaries with children.

If our children, as they become adults, decide to no longer have a relationship with us, that is something we need to respect. Again, I am making the worst-case scenario, as that would be a heavy ordeal to grieve. Our children will, without our permission, make their own mistakes. We have to trust, if we raised our children to be healthy, that they will try to have healthy relationships. Our influence is only useful for as long as our children feel it is useful. It is not up to us as parents to decide what is right or wrong for our adult children. The values and morals of healthy relationships were designed to be taught when they were younger. If you have children that have cut you out or have limited you, it is likely due to your limited awareness as a parent. If you truly believe that you are an authentic person who cares deeply about communication and honest conversation with your child, you will have to patiently wait for your child to open their life up to you again. We cannot make our children love us or value us. They have to do that themselves. Children need healthy lines and boundaries and a massive amount of education on family morals, values, beliefs, and ideologies. If these are not clearly articulated at home, or the child feels that those values do not fit them, they will create boundaries with you as a parent. I will say, almost no child wants to have to say goodbye to living parents. Most children have tried everything to make their parents love them. Love does not mean "all-accepting" or "all-harmonious," *but it does mean clarification and understanding of one another, even if values don't match.*

Ryan has a strained relationship with his parents. He is 23 years old and lives with his girlfriend Mindy. They both went to the same college and graduated together. They both work in the same marketing firm now. Ryan decided he didn't want to follow his dad into the family business, which caused a riff in the family. Ryan has tried to explain to his dad that the carpentry business is not something he wants to make a career out of. He has told him he has worked at the family business his whole life and really wanted to find a career that was his and one that he enjoyed. His dad had the expectation for Ryan's entire childhood that he would be the man to take over the family business. This devastated Ryan's dad and now Ryan's dad has been bitter ever since. He doesn't call him anymore, he barely says two words during holidays, and he comments on Ryan's career at every family dinner. Mindy has known about this issue their entire relationship. After a family birthday party dinner Mindy says to Ryan, "I really just think you need to consider your dad's offer. I mean, you only get one dad and you don't want to keep disappointing him do you? It is not like you're really giving up that much, right? Also he can pay you better than you get paid now! It really sounds like a win-win."

Do you think Mindy has a good point? How do you think Ryan feels after hearing Mindy say this? Does Ryan need to look at what it means to attend family events or have another conversation with his dad? What boundaries does Ryan need to make with either Mindy or his parents or both?

*SEE APPENDIX FOR A POTENTIAL SPIRITUAL ABUSE PITFALL FOR THIS SECTION.

CHAPTER FIVE

FRIENDS

~~~~~~

I am sure you have heard the phrase "friends come and go." Yes, I do believe this is true. I think very few friendships last longer than a decade, and most friendships are seasonal. If this isn't the case for you, congratulations—but you're likely an outlier. Friendships are probably one of the easiest and hardest to make boundaries within because they are the family you choose. Why did you choose them? Well, typically we choose friends because they are like us or they have qualities we want to be more like. Our goal as healthy humans is to find other healthy humans to be friends with. Healthy humans fulfill our lives. They make us feel wanted, important, loved, and can sometimes be better family than our families of origin. They can fall away with time and distance, which is always sad, or they can thrive with us in life and join us in our adventures and life transitions. Friends should feel like a home away from home. They just know you so well; they know what to say to make everything better. (Or to just prove that you were obviously right about that stupid coworker!) They have our backs, they show up, they are reliable, they say sorry, and they show you they care—unless they don't. What do we do when they don't?

Brené Brown has a book called *Rising Strong*. Her seven characteristics of trust are just true. They are spot on the money. They are BRAVING: Boundaries, Reliability, Accountability, Vault (keeping secrets), Integrity, Non-Judgment, and Generosity (Brown, 2015, pp. 199–200). Friends typically fulfill—along with hopefully spouses—

all this anatomy of a trusting relationship. These are self-explanatory, but if you want to read more about them, it is never a bad idea to pick up a Brené Brown book. Trust is the bedrock of any relationship. It made the most sense to me to discuss trust in this chapter because friendships are the relationships we have the most practice in. We have the most practice in ending and making new friends. We can't really end a mom or dad relationship and just pick a new one up with someone else, nor with siblings, really. Frankly, with spouses, some people do that, but it is massively expensive to keep trying to restart those relationships. Trust is the most **basic** place to start when making friends. As adults, we often have a hard time making friends, but a fun secret to this is: Just be a trustworthy person. Sounds insane, I know, but it feels like so many people aren't. Allegedly, being a trustworthy person is as impressive as knowing rocket science. That is goofy to me, but I think we may all know someone who falls into this untrustworthy category.

Right, the question remains, what if they don't prove trustworthy? If said friend is not upholding the basic fundamentals of friendship, it is most likely a problem within these seven principles. Typically, they aren't reliable anymore, refuse to apologize for anything, have horrible boundaries, are judgy toward you, don't have strong beliefs and shift on them frequently, or are hypercritical of everything you do and don't really see things from your side—or refuse to. These are often the places where a friendship breaks down. This is where we need boundaries.

Often the conversation will start with something like, "It is really hard for me to feel like I can depend on you when you constantly tell me you will be at my house, but then ten minutes before you are supposed to be here, you bail. I feel like I am really not a valuable friend to you." This is not a bad boundary to have! Unpredictability is really hurtful to some people, and it doesn't bother others. My point is that you are allowed to be bothered by this. No one likes to feel that they are deprioritized or that their time is wasted by someone who didn't think twice about dropping them. We go back to the logic that healthy people are okay with boundaries and unhealthy people are not. A healthy friend in this situation would respond with, "Oh, my gosh, you are right. I have done that the last couple of months! That is so bad of me. I am struggling with this. I will definitely get better at that. I really don't want you feeling like you are not a priority. You are! I will fix that." Then they actually do. Unhealthy people get defensive and get mad at you for their behavior. That's weird in the logical world. I behave poorly toward you, and somehow that is your fault? Yeah, that doesn't make sense.

Friendships are often the area we practice setting boundaries in the most. If they are healthy, you will get an idea of what good lines of boundaries are and what are not. I do encourage people to be very picky with their friendships. It is not your job to be everybody's friend. You do not want everyone to like you. That just makes you an emotional slave to everyone else's definition of friendship. That is a nightmare. It is your job to know your definition of a good friend and **be** that good friend. At that point, we don't tolerate those who aren't willing to reciprocate the support we offer them. Friends can be just as emotionally draining as any family member. Maintain firm boundaries for yourself and remember that true friends like the real you. They want you to be honest with them. They want to know when they hurt you so they don't do it again. Even if your values and those of your friends are different, respecting each other's needs shouldn't be painful, sacrificial, or impossible to maintain.

FRIENDSHIPS ARE OFTEN THE AREA WE PRACTICE SETTING BOUNDARIES IN THE MOST. IF THEY ARE HEALTHY, YOU WILL GET AN IDEA OF WHAT GOOD LINES OF BOUNDARIES ARE AND WHAT ARE NOT. I DO ENCOURAGE PEOPLE TO BE VERY PICKY WITH THEIR FRIENDSHIPS.

Rebecca and Carrie are friends from work. They both clicked really easily since Rebecca started working at Carrie's law firm, and now they go to lunch almost every day together. Carrie just finished winning her litigation and it really impressed one of the partners. It is possible they have their eye on Carrie to become a partner in the firm after this win. Rebecca is very excited for Carrie but Carrie seems to think that Rebecca is competition now. Carrie starts slowly backing away from Rebecca. She doesn't show up to lunch as much anymore, she is working more hours than Rebecca, and in meetings Carrie always has a retort against a statement that Rebecca makes. Rebecca starts to notice this change and isn't sure how to handle it. She wants to talk to Carrie but she also feels a bit threatened and put off by her behavior. Rebecca is in an uncomfortable spot because she feels like she doesn't belong at work the same way she used to, and also feels like she is getting alienated and called out frequently. Rebecca still acts cordial to Carrie, but Carrie sees this as weakness and tries to take advantage of it. Carrie starts talking about Rebecca's past legal mistakes, how she was late to turn in a file to the magistrate which caused a delay, and how she isn't as timely as other staff members in email responses back to clients. Rebecca has to decide how to go about balancing work and her shifted relationship with Carrie.

What decisions has Carrie made about Rebecca? What are some of Rebecca's options? If Rebecca were to ask you how to handle Carrie what would you say?

*SEE APPENDIX FOR A POTENTIAL SPIRITUAL ABUSE PITFALL FOR THIS SECTION.

CHAPTER SIX

SAVIOR COMPLEX

∼∼∼∼∼∼∼∼∼∼∼∼∼∼∼∼∼∼∼∼∼∼∼∼∼∼∼∼∼∼∼∼∼

L et's look into the fact that so many of you think you live in the Harry Potter books. It really is wild to me how much power people believe they have. I think the biggest issue is that people think they have the ability to control or change people. This is utterly ridiculous on a logical level. I don't know about the rest of you, but I cannot get my own cat to pick me as the favorite human of the house. I'm the spare human at best and will instantly get abandoned when the favorite human comes home. I can't even control my cat! You know what else would be awesome to control? My plants' growth. Yup, I would love to figure out why they die on me all the time. Why can't I just control their growth? What is wrong with me! I should be able to control the weather too while I'm at it! Forget that predictions have a 30% accuracy overall, and those weather people still have their job. We can't even predict the weather accurately, so who thinks they can control it? It is so incredibly ridiculous to assume that you have the power to control anything external. We even have a hard time controlling our own bodies! They get sick on us all the time. We didn't warrant that behavior! How dare it! What is our body doing fighting against us? The faster you realize how little you actually control in the world, the easier this concept is when applied to other people.

So, then your logic is, "But I can change them!" What? You have gone how many years trying to change someone so they will treat you like a person? Nothing has worked so far. You think you are that magical? You actually believe you have the power to change another human? That is next-level magic. That is what the Imperius Curse is in Harry Potter (Rowling, 2000)! You think you can magically wave your wand and make them love you and show up for you and be what you need? That would be some *serious* magical abilities. People's decisions—listen carefully—are their own. You have *zero*, zilch, nada influence on a person's decision about what you mean to them. You're not the one who gets to determine whether you're a good person. It's others who assess whether you're a good spouse, parent, friend, sibling, and so on. You can't simply decide for yourself if you're "good" in any given role. For instance, if you're a sibling, it's your siblings who define whether you're a good one, not you. After all, you can't be a sibling to yourself, so you lack the perspective to make that judgment.

Armed with this insight, we can examine the judgments and decisions that others have already made concerning us. A crucial aspect of setting boundaries involves acknowledging and respecting the perceptions others hold of us. If someone holds a negative view of you, then their actions toward you will likely reflect that perception. It's as straightforward as that. The fundamental logic underlying this concept is quite simple: *The way others treat you is a reflection of how they perceive you.* Therefore, it's essential to honor and accept how you're treated, while also taking people at their word when they express their thoughts about themselves and about you. This message is essential to absorb as it is one of the most pivotal points I can convey about navigating relationships with others. Believe them.

It is necessary that you grieve the belief that you have any say or control over any other person than yourself. It is your job to be the best version of yourself and make sure you are teaching healthy morals and principles to your children so they can thrive in life. However, when a child gets to an adult age and makes clear to you that you have not been good to them, you need to hear them and respect that and not guilt them into thinking they owe you anything. Welcome to the rest of society where no one—not even your kids—owes you **anything**.

Here we go with, "But it's your mom! But it's your dad! But it's your brother/sister!" Who cares? Seriously, that means anyone in the whole world can abuse you because of some label. That is a logical fallacy. If you make excuses for parents, you need to make an excuse for everyone else—that they are also not responsible for their treatment of others. You cannot excuse people for hurting you or others. It is amazing to me that people don't realize that if you are an adult with unhealthy parents, you are both *legal adults*. If you and your father go in and steal something from the store, do you seriously think that because "it is your dad" that they will get a lesser sentence and consequence than you? Absolutely not! You as an adult are equally responsible for all your own choices as they are theirs. *There isn't an excuse for abuse.* You are the only one granting permission for people to continue to hurt and harm you.

YOU CAN'T SAVE PEOPLE. YOU CAN HELP PEOPLE, BUT YOU CAN'T SAVE THEM. YOU CAN'T CHANGE SOMEONE'S PERSPECTIVE UNLESS THEY ARE WILLING TO ABSORB WHAT IT IS YOU ARE SAYING TO THEM.

You can't save people. You can help people, but you can't save them. You can't change someone's perspective unless they are willing to absorb what it is you are saying to them. Most people cannot absorb your help at certain points in their life because they are unwilling or unready to hear it. Knowing that you have done everything in your power—and you are really not that powerful—is one of the most relieving feelings to have. It is not your job. It is not your responsibility to make decisions for anyone else. You can't make anyone feel anything. You are not that powerful. Please come to terms with your humanness. You are a person. Please realize you are only a person, nothing more, nothing less.

Larry always saves his friends. When all of his friends go out to the bar Larry is always the designated driver. He is seen as the dad of the group and is nicknamed "Daddy Larry." When going out drinking one of his friends, Mark, gets in one of his angry drunk stages again. Mark likes to pick fights with other men sometimes and this time he broke a bottle over the bar, kicked several stools down, and got thrown out. He tried to gain re-entry into the bar but the bouncer pulled him out of the doorway. This caused the police to show up and Mark gets taken off to jail for the night. Larry is currently in a bit of debt. He co-signed with his other friend Jim so Jim could get an apartment and Jim backslid on a payment which caused Larry to have to take out another credit card. His other friend Kevin is living with him because he lost his job and had no where to go, but doesn't make Kevin pay rent, and he has already been living there for three months. He is dating a girl who really values him for always paying for all their meals and any shopping she likes to do. Larry is now having to bail Mark out of jail again and his bail this time is another $250 and Mark has never paid Larry back for his past bail outs. Larry is starting to get tired and a bit agitated with everyone around him lately. He notices it, but still keeps pushing through to always show up for his friends.

How has Larry's savior complex affected him? Do you think Larry has a good balance in his life? Do you think Larry feels he has to save everyone to be respected?

*SEE APPENDIX FOR A POTENTIAL SPIRITUAL ABUSE PITFALL FOR THIS SECTION.

CHAPTER SEVEN

HOW TO GRIEVE

~~~~~~

Grieving is essentially crying: it's the expression of emotional pain. Yes, it's uncomfortable and unpleasant, but so is the process of healing in any context. When you visit the doctor for stitches, you anticipate discomfort and itching during the healing process, don't you? Healing, whether emotional or physical, invariably involves discomfort and pain. If emotions are wounded, they require healing, which entails pain. Similarly, when a bone is broken, it necessitates healing, accompanied by inconvenience and pain. Healing is inherently painful. We all possess an innate understanding of how to grieve. Just watch a young child who scrapes their knee and begins to cry—it's a natural response to pain. Unlike our physical bodies, we can suppress and bury our emotions, but they inevitably resurface with even greater intensity at a later, often inconvenient, time. You can't instruct your body to halt the healing process like you can with emotions. However, attempting to suppress emotional responses only leads to a more forceful resurgence of those suppressed feelings.

Megan Devine, Elisabeth Kübler-Ross, and Mary-Frances O'Conner have written books on grieving.[4] What I like about Devine is that she is very validating about expressing grief and how it works. She clearly appreciates the fact that so many people don't know what to say to

---

[4]"It's OK that You're Not OK" by Megan Devine
For Kübler-Ross resources see footnote 2
"The Grieving Brain" by Mary-Frances O'Connor

others when they are grieving and gives encouraging statements on how to listen to what is helpful and what is not. So many people don't know what to do with grief that they end up shaming anyone who feels sad. I believe that is outward admittance of emotional immaturity, and more people should be embarrassed by that. Another helpful way to look at grief is through stages. Kübler-Ross addresses five stages she labels: Denial, Bargaining, Anger, Sadness, Acceptance (Kübler-Ross, 2005). She states that they do not necessarily appear in this order —that they can be in any order—but these are standard hallmarks to hit during grief. O'Conner has a background in neuroscience if you are interested in learning more about the process the brain organically takes you through, she provides a great outline for that.

Grieving entails facing the most agonizing aspects of loss head-on and allowing yourself to experience the pain. I've witnessed the profound transformation that occurs when one fully embraces their emotions. It's truly remarkable. Nothing quite shifts someone's perspective and understanding of the world as swiftly and profoundly as allowing oneself to grieve authentically. I observe this phenomenon in action regularly. The difference in how someone communicates before and after allowing themselves to feel the depths of their grief is astounding. Their perspective, sense of self, and comprehension of the world undergo significant changes. However, I often find myself needing to point out this shift to them, which suggests that most may not recognize it on their own. Engaging in activities such as journaling about the most painful aspects of your experience, allowing yourself to cry wholeheartedly, and then reflecting upon your emotions can be incredibly enlightening. Pay close attention to how your language and perception evolve throughout this process. While the reality of the situation remains unchanged, it is perceived and processed differently within us.

Have faith in your body's innate ability to heal. Just as it effortlessly repairs a scrape or a mystery bruise, it is equally capable of tending to your emotional wounds. Your role is simply to allow your emotions the space to fulfill their purpose. Think of it like the control panel in the headquarters of your mind, as depicted in the movie *Inside Out*:

Sometimes, it's Sadness's turn to take the lead and navigate through the complexities of your inner world. Trust that when sadness has served its purpose, it will gracefully step aside, ready for the next emotion to guide the way.

EFFECTIVE GRIEVING INVOLVES CONFRONTING AND PROCESSING EMOTIONS IN A CONSTRUCTIVE MANNER, RATHER THAN BECOMING ENSNARED IN IRRATIONAL DESPAIR.

If you struggle with depression, this isn't the right advice for you. Depression often manifests in the form of deeply ingrained beliefs about oneself and the world. Individuals grappling with depression may find themselves trapped in cycles of intense emotion, frequently spiraling over unresolved issues. This repetitive pattern can become a relentless cycle of anguish without resolution. Effective grieving involves confronting and processing emotions in a constructive manner, rather than becoming ensnared in irrational despair. Consider, for instance, someone lamenting their perceived ugliness. By assigning a subjective label without a concrete definition, they perpetuate a self-fulfilling prophecy of sorrow. This circular reasoning solidifies the notion of their ugliness as an immutable truth, leaving little room for healing or growth. Once a subjective perception takes root, it becomes extremely difficult to challenge, as it is based solely on personal interpretation rather than objective reality. In essence, choosing to cling to such beliefs perpetuates a state of sadness devoid of reason or escape. This often needs extra support. If this is a persistent pattern for you, then seek out the help you need from a trained professional you trust.

Once you let the pain do its job—and, frankly, it can take a very long time—there are profound perspective shifts that occur. Especially in our most cherished relationships, it's not uncommon to spend years grieving certain circumstances or dynamics that we needed for our own growth and fulfillment. This isn't abnormal, just a natural progression. Letting your emotions do their job gifts us with maturity, logic, realism, and a path forward. We obtain the ability to perceive others' understanding of us as it truly exists, free from our own desires and expectations. This newfound clarity is not clouded or muddied by what we desire, need, want, or wish. It just is. This is often accompanied by peace, understanding, and a change in our self-perspective that we were not able to see before. Adapting to this new worldview can be challenging and will require intentional work on your emotional state. I have never met anyone who has regretted grieving. It is odd, isn't it? Isn't it intriguing how the very thing we often avoid holds such profound value for our personal growth? Don't sabotage yourself; embrace the pain, for it gives you the power to see yourself more clearly.

~~~~~~~~~~~~~~~~~~~~~~~~~~~~~~~

Probably the most important part of crying is to make sure you get a good night's sleep! This is **so** vital. Sleep causes the brain to file data into the correct memory banks it needs to. Furthermore, "The dream state also facilitates plastic change . . . REM sleep seems necessary for neurons to grow normally. REM sleep has also been shown to be particularly important for enhancing our ability to retain emotional memories and for allowing the hippocampus to turn short-term memories of the day before into long-term ones (i.e., it helps make memories more permanent, leading to structural change in the brain)" (Doidge, 2007, pp. 239–40). This is why we feel refreshed when we get a good night's sleep. So, trust that your exhaustion is taking you to a natural state of sleep after a good cry. It takes a very long time, like a painfully long time, to get through something if you don't sleep well after you grieve. If you notice that you have cried at all throughout your day, you have to make sleep a priority—ideally more than you normally would. I typically say try for 8 to 10 hours and let your body wake up naturally for the most idyllic way to make sure your grief is getting filed correctly in your brain. *You must prioritize sleep when you are grieving!*

Another major rule for grieving well is do it alone or only with safe people. Do not share this depth of yourself with unsafe people. This will cause your mind to think that being sad is bad when it is not—it is just that the other person doesn't know how to handle their own sadness, so they project it onto you. Shaming you for feeling sad has *nothing to do with you* and everything to do with them. It is typically best to cry alone unless you have a really emotionally safe and mature person who knows how to hold all those complex emotions in the air for you. Unsafe people will make you feel bad for being a human. There is that logic again!

A common question is: But do I tell them I am cutting them out? Do I tell them all these things that have hurt me? Do I just straight tell them? My question back to you is: Haven't you already? If you haven't, is it because you have tried and got beaten down so hard emotionally and verbally you never thought to do it again? My word for this is "absorbability." Not everyone is able to absorb the information that you are telling them. Some people cannot and refuse to hear what you are saying about them. Therefore, you go through all this effort and time and lay all the issues out like your own personal intervention letter, you put your heart and soul into this and why it matters so much to you—and they don't care or they blame you. I believe you have the data you need to make this decision already. If you are just dealing with someone who has toxic traits, and you think they can absorb what you are saying, then tell them! If you are avoiding it, the question is: Is it for a legit reason? Is the reason that you don't like conflict? If it is the latter, then that is an issue you have to sort out. The reality is, conflict is already here! If this weren't a problem, it wouldn't be bothering you so much—so you are actually extending conflict by hiding behind "people pleasing." That's a maturity issue on your end. Let's not electively abuse ourselves into believing that what we have to say is going to be heard and absorbed by the other person if we know them to be unable to absorb our message. Some people can **never** understand you. It is, again, not your job to make someone understand. This is an essential point because if you keep being vulnerable to people who beat you over the head with it—you are now abusing yourself.

NOW, HERE IS THE HARD TRUTH WHEN IT COMES TO GRIEVING THE LIVING IN GENERAL. NO ONE IS COMING TO SAVE YOU. NOTHING CAN SAVE YOU FROM THIS PAIN. YOU *CAN* AVOID IT! HOWEVER, THAT DOES COME WITH ITS OWN CONSEQUENCES. YOU ARE GOING INTO A DEEP EMOTIONAL OCEAN OF STORMS, AND IT WILL TAKE TIME BEFORE YOU COME OUT OKAY.

Now, here is the hard truth when it comes to grieving the living in general. No one is coming to save you. Nothing can save you from this pain. You *can* avoid it! However, that does come with its own consequences. You are going into a deep emotional ocean of storms, and it will take time before you come out okay. Be gentle with yourself and expect healing for a long time. Do not sugar coat this with such thoughts as, "This is so easy!" or "It's not that bad!" You will lie to yourself and cause self-betrayal issues in the process. You need to know this is incredibly painful. You must go through this pain alone. No one will be able to understand your pain the way you understand your pain. People say the most hurtful statements to us during grief, whether that is over a death or in grieving a relationship. It is not their job to save you or even validate you. I wouldn't expect it. I would honestly expect for others to hurt you more. It is your job to take ahold of your grief and move through this storm. You are the only you there is, and the things you will be grieving are very different than things other people will be grieving. Few people are helpful in our grief. That's why grieving with safe people is so important, if you are blessed enough to have them. If they do help you, that's amazing. However, they can't ever truly understand your specific pain. Pain in relationships is unique because there is no one like you, and no one is like them. If you feel like your emotions are too overwhelming, you are doing it right. It is supposed to feel like a deep despair with that scary angler fish in the depths. Don't worry, you don't get lost down here—but if it feels like you are, you're on the right path.

I have never in my life heard someone say "I really hate the fact that I emotionally dealt with my pain." I know way more people who have regretted **not** grieving and even have hurt themselves or attempted a more permanent solution to try to avoid grieving. No one can cry themselves to death. Not that I have ever heard, anyway. So, allow your brain to do the healing work it needs to do to get you to the other side of the sadness. To tell yourself you are not strong enough to handle emotions really is a disservice to your abilities. We are literally designed to heal. Our brains and bodies work so hard to help us heal all the time. It is supposed to feel like a deep dark hole; it is supposed to feel like no one will love you again. Of course, none of that is actually true, but it needs to *feel* like it in order for your brain to do its job. Too many people are afraid of their own emotions, and it is a detriment to our society and relationships. It is destructive to hold onto grief and not heal it and blame everyone else for something we are afraid of. Grief will not kill you; sadness will not destroy you, but it will feel like hell. Healing is always painful. The more you avoid the pain, the more destructive it becomes.

This process takes an immense amount of self-discipline. The reluctance to have self-discipline and grieve over the most painful parts of the goodbye is why people are dysregulated for long periods of time. It is, again, like any other skill set. If you want to work out, you must make time for it and be self-disciplined; if you want to learn piano, you must be self-disciplined; if you want to learn a sport, be self-disciplined. Grieving is not an exception. Grieving well has sadly turned into a learned skill set, even though we are naturally designed to do it. Our American society gives us too many inaccurate messages about grief and its unimportance. It seems to take a long time to move through perceiving ourselves as "weak" or "pitiful" before we can actually handle the emotional state. It is a lie to think you are weak for maturely handling your emotions. Going back to the effort it takes—it's a skill set. You must be a mess for a long time before you can present yourself as someone skilled in discussing their own grief. No one just starting to work out competes in body building until it is time; people have piano *rehearsals* for a reason before they show others what they have practiced. This is why the skill set of grieving well is necessary to do safely alone for a while until you can handle expressing this grief to others. The articulation comes with time—and being a mess. It doesn't just **happen**. This is where that people logic comes back into place. Growing in grief takes time, sadness, and being a puddle on the floor sometimes.

A lot of people say, "This is too hard." Yes, it is. That is the point. That is why we cry. The pain is too much and too hard. That's why we need to feel it. One of the ways people try to avoid the inevitable pain is to say, "I went through the grief process already! I already cried once! I already got mad a couple of times!" I mean, that is like saying, "What do you mean I am not a famous piano player yet? I already practiced...like, twice!" That is really goofy. If you had actually moved through the grief, you wouldn't be trying to convince others, or even yourself, you have already done the work. When someone has done the grief work, it is glaringly obvious. Their language changes, their understanding is different, and the way they speak about the subject and even their view on others shifts. When someone is well-practiced in something—it shows. It is that simple. If you are avoiding the grief—that is also glaringly obvious. A lot of people don't realize that when you are **not** a self-aware person, you tell people everything they need to know about you. You say it. You treat them a certain way, you talk about yourself a certain way, your behaviors are specific to your situation. It is clear to see what emotional work people have done based on observing their basic behavior and speech. I have been told that observation of people's language is a skill you have to learn—sure. But once you see it in someone, you can't really unsee it. Once you hear how people speak about other people, once you watch how people behave, they tell you **so much** about themselves unintentionally. If you believe that you have already *done the work* and have gone through the pain—that will be obvious.

Another fun area to address is the excuse, "Everyone grieves differently! So, this isn't the only way to do it!" This is a fun mixture of truthful and untruthful statements. Yes, the process of grief looks different for everyone. Some people need to run, paint, journal, have a sad playlist in the car, take a bath, or go on vacation. The methodology you pick and feel the most connected to yourself in does not have to be a "correct" behavior. The point is that you **feel** the pain that you need to feel, regardless of how you get to that emotional state. It is true that everyone has their own way of reaching that emotional state, but the pain is not different. You must be self-disciplined in getting yourself to that place of **feeling through** your pain. There are a ton of options to get there, but you cannot use one method and call it "grieving" when, for example, that vacation you took was to run away from your grief. One person's method for reaching the pain is not the same as another's—that's true. The point is getting to this emotional destination the way you know will let you process the sadness.

If you are having a hard time eliciting the emotions, some common mantras I have heard that seem to really help people are phrases like: "You are loved, even if they don't love you." "I matter, even if I am the only person who tells myself that." "This isn't the end of my story." "You are worth this fight because your journey isn't over." "Some people can come with you in life, and some people can't, and that is not your fault." "I need people in my life who want to grow with me, not hold me back." These are just some ideas to help you reach the emotional beliefs you want to achieve. You know you picked a good mantra if it feels like it punches you in the gut and makes you tear up.

Healthy people want you to hold true and authentic thoughts and beliefs about yourself. They want to encourage you to be the best you. Unhealthy people are happy to use you the way you best benefit them. Don't let them make decisions for you. Say goodbye to the toxic pieces of a relationship or even people that can't come with you on your path forward. Even a tree needs the dead branches cut off to grow. If the branches stay, the tree is stunted.

> # HEALTHY PEOPLE WANT YOU TO HOLD TRUE AND AUTHENTIC THOUGHTS AND BELIEFS ABOUT YOURSELF. THEY WANT TO ENCOURAGE YOU TO BE THE BEST YOU. UNHEALTHY PEOPLE ARE HAPPY TO USE YOU THE WAY YOU BEST BENEFIT THEM. DON'T LET THEM MAKE DECISIONS FOR YOU.

Once you finish your grief process, it doesn't come back up or feel the same way—that is how you know you are moving through it. **It is measurable!** You can tell if you feel different about a topic or subject after you have cried about it.

You are not "weak" for taking care of your emotions to prevent them from hurting other people. That is the opposite of weak. Weak people are in denial of their issues and hurt people to avoid taking responsibility for how they hurt people. Don't let this be you because you lack self-discipline. This is where I often get the most pushback. I tend to get a lot of stubborn responses here. Favorites include: "Well, I don't want to." "It doesn't feel good." "It is too hard." "It means that the sadness is real." These are some of the most illogical emotional reasons, and they come off as irrational. If you don't want to, then keep hurting people! Those are your options. "It doesn't feel good." Sure! But why do you think so? "It means the sadness is real." When was the sadness fake? It has been real the entire time, anyway! You are just not dealing with it. These are defense mechanisms that prolong the pain. Prioritize maturity—grieve the pieces you need to so that you stop hurting yourself and others for longer than you already have. There is no excuse for you not taking control of your emotional state. If you keep denying your responsibility for this pain, you are no different than the person(s) you are setting boundaries for that are handing you the consequences of their pain. If you want to be just like the people you need boundaries with, then this book is useless to you.

CONSEQUENCES OF NOT GRIEVING

Grieving is a root issue. When you look at emotions, some are known as root emotions and others are more superficial in nature. Most evidence I have seen indicates that there are four common emotional consequences for not grieving. When we avoid grief, it tends to show up as anger, anxiety, numbness, and toxic positivity. A lot of people who avoid grief seem to fall into these four categories. Typically, anger shows up for those who have a strong advocacy side. Anxiety shows up for those who care deeply about being preventative from bad things happening. Those who are numb to the world try to protect people from themselves because they feel out of control. Toxic positivity seems to show up in people who care about making everyone happy. Sometimes all four! For a lot of people, their anger will show up in every relationship around them. Not only are they putting themselves in no-win situations, but they put everyone else around them in no-wins as well. Those with anxiety tend to amp it up on the perfectionistic side, i.e., "Nothing I ever do is good enough" or the debilitating side, i.e., "What if I never recover from this?" They tend to get hyper controlling as well and want to know every detail about everything. Those who numb out keep people at arm's length and don't allow for closeness to happen in their relationships. Those who embrace toxic positivity tend to act like nothing is wrong and put on a face of happiness without any genuine connection to the feeling. I think people who fall on the toxic positivity side **think** they are doing a good job convincing people they are fine, but everyone around them can tell, and they end up pushing people away in the process because it comes off disingenuous and fake. There is not a single way that these emotions don't rub off on people around you. Everyone in your life will be able to tell you are "off" or that something isn't right. A lot of people in this stage use the phrase, "I am feeling very unsettled." For your first guess on emotions, ask yourself: What are you avoiding? What are you not wanting to deal with? What is too painful for you to handle right now? These questions will typically get you to the right answer or a closer answer. You will know when you identify it. The whole body reacts and settles into the reality of what is being avoided.

I want to make a warning about not healing well. If you do not heal well, the consequences show up rather quickly in other relationships in your life. People will often report to you that they don't feel safe around you, connected to you, and/or your relationship is suffering. Why? Great question! When you have grief, your perspective on a lot of the world around you shifts. Think about a fight you had with a significant other. If you think back about how you viewed the world during that time, you might be able to see how decisions and relationships were affected. For example, I had a colleague after grad school who broke up with her boyfriend after 4 years. The problem was she kept refusing to deal with how sad she was. She kept attempting to go along with her life as if she hadn't skipped a beat. She kept saying she was fine, things were going well with her, and she felt good. I can appreciate the attempt to have her focus on her work, but it was clear she wasn't dealing with this outside of work either. Coworkers started to notice her get angry easily and get hyper-controlling. This is an example of how the beginning stages look. What happens when you still don't address it? The feelings tend to evolve. As I discussed earlier, the most common evolutions I have interacted with are anger, anxiety, numbness, and toxic positivity. When we are constantly defensive or angry, that will show up quickly with those around us. If we are already more anxiety-prone, we tend to panic quicker or spike our perfectionism. If we don't want to feel our feelings, people prone to addiction often pick up a drug of choice to avoid the pain of grieving or decide to dissociate and go numb, resulting in a robotic communication style. Toxic positive people who are clearly forcing themselves to see the bright side of things are difficult to have a genuine relationship with because they dismiss and belittle any concerns.

FEAR CAUSES OUR BRAIN TO MAKE DECISIONS IT WOULDN'T OTHERWISE MAKE WHEN WE ARE SCARED. FEAR IS VERY POWERFUL. FEAR EXISTS FOR OUR SURVIVAL, SO OUR BRAIN PRIORITIZES THIS EMOTION TO PROTECT US.

Why do we choose these scary and toxic behaviors over healing? Fear. Fear of what will be found upon searching the depths of our emotions, fear of what others will think about the emotions or our reactions, or fear that we simply won't be able to find an answer or peace. As we discussed previously, boundaries are often necessary when we desire love that another will not, or cannot, give us. It is scary to think that we are not loved. Fear causes our brain to make decisions it wouldn't otherwise make when we are scared. Fear is very powerful. Fear exists for our survival, so our brain prioritizes this emotion to protect us. What happens when fear overrides healing? That's right, you self-sabotage.

CHAPTER EIGHT

THE OTHER SIDE

Once you have allowed your pain to overcome you, and you are past being a puddle on the floor with the burrito blanket feeling as though the covers have accepted you as one of their own, new feelings emerge. These new feelings typically start out kind of numbed. It is often a disillusioned feeling that this actually is my reality. Welcome to step one of being on the other side! It should feel as stressful and disorienting as stepping off a plane at a new airport and looking for directions. While this feeling is most common, you could experience just about any emotion under the "acceptance" stage. Here, reality hits, and we have a lot to learn or relearn. There is going to be a lot of new territory here for you emotionally, especially if you have never had to cut someone out of your life or limit their closeness to you.

I am an unfriendly human and an odd duck—in the sense that cutting people out of my life is relatively easy—but I have practice in it. I am a sensitive soul, believe it or not, and I can't invest emotions in people who can't treat me like a basic human. If that treatment ends, then they have to go—because I know I can't keep people in my life who don't love me. I demand it of people. If you are going to be in my life, you will start by treating me like a person and hold yourself to a high standard or you're out. I am sharing this because one of the next phases following the fog is realizing that you have a much clearer understanding of what you need from others. It is often incredibly easy to identify at this point. It is also easy to articulate so people never have to guess what you want from them. It is a very transparent relationship.

Embracing transparency empowers you to live authentically like never before! That is worth more than gold in my opinion. To never have to hide, try, attempt, convey, sway, or control another human to love you ever again is so incredibly freeing.

The beauty of free-will love is that it is all elective choice. People are electively choosing you—to love you—every single day just because they feel like it and want to. That's kind of amazing. No one has an obligation to love you. No one has to feel manipulated into doing things for anyone ever again. This is one of the most liberating feelings I think a person can possibly have. It is like being released from student loan debt or your mortgage! That feeling you got just now when I said that, yeah, that's the goal for you to feel every single day about yourself and your relationships. No more carrying around your griefcase!

This stage has a different kind of grief—I call it grieving the good. I love how you thought the grief was over! "Grieving the good" is the process of acknowledging and appreciating all the remarkable qualities about people and yourself that you may not have previously recognized or fully understood. For a lot of people, it is learning yourself again and realizing that you are **not** in a state of survival. The brain functions very differently in surviving than it does in thriving, and our neurochemistry has to adjust accordingly. We have to learn who we are when we are not just surviving. Toxic relationships force us into a fight/flight/freeze/fawn responses because we are communal creatures. Whether we introverts like it or not, we are social mammals, and we need other humans even if we hate that that is true. We need them because being abandoned by your pack is life-threatening. When wolves leave a wounded wolf behind, that wolf knows it means death. Your brain, as well, interprets abandonment as a life-threatening situation. It is why we simp, if you will, so hard for people to love us and develop really scary people pleasing behaviors and are willing to sacrifice all of who we are so they will love us.

Who are you without merely surviving your relationships? That's a new life, I bet. What if you are in a place where you never actually have to survive another relationship ever again? Maybe because your boundaries and communicating those boundaries are so good? This means that you will need to learn who you are when you are thriving. This is a different part of our brain, and it only comes out when we feel **completely safe**. Thriving is only possible in safety. Make it a priority to make all relationships emotionally safe in your life.

OUR BRAIN HAS A WAY OF MAKING US THINK WE ARE NOT SAFE WHEN WE ARE SAFE. THIS IS BECAUSE FEAR IS ONE OF THE STRONGEST EMOTIONS WE CAN HAVE. OUR BRAIN IS DESIGNED TO KEEP US ALIVE. IT WILL REACH FOR THINGS TO BE AFRAID OF WHEN WE ARE USED TO BEING, WELL, AFRAID.

Once you are safe and have clearly established and can clearly communicate what those emotional boundaries in safety are, you get the fun part of starting to explore things you may have never had the opportunity to explore before! You may remember us talking about the safety–fun effect earlier. Our brain has a way of making us think we are not safe when we are safe. This is because fear is one of the strongest emotions we can have. Our brain is designed to keep us alive. It will reach for things to be afraid of when we are used to being, well, afraid. Luckily, this doesn't actually last long in real time, but it does feel like a very lost place to be.

It is always easiest to start small. These small decisions that you start realizing will come together, and decisions about your preferences become easier and easier. It is really sad that a lot of times in our unhealthy relationships we were never asked such simple questions! "What do you like? Do you have a preference? What do you think of this thing?" The language a lot of us are used to hearing is, "Why is it so hard for you to make a decision? You know I don't like that place! You know how I feel about that outfit you are wearing! You really don't look good in that!" These are frequent statements that we are ready to defend ourselves against! It is weird to think that in a healthy relationship, you will not have a negative opinion shot at you for making your own decisions. It's a new world, where people kind of don't care what your preferences are, they are just happy to have you around. They just want you to like what you decide! Learning more about yourself is a confusing journey, but the best part about it is...you are allowed to be wrong. You are allowed to be wrong about something you *think* you like. If you pick something and go, "Hmm, I thought I liked this, but I don't actually think I do," no one will be mad at you! No one will blame you for that! It is odd. But healthy people will treat you the way you as a healthy person treat them! You've never thought about giving a judgmental opinion on someone you love, have you? I bet you haven't really noticed or cared to comment on their preferences unless they were exceptionally flattering or unflattering. That's the proof in the pudding. If you haven't noticed it about others, others likely won't notice it about you!

I bring this up in particular because this was a very jarring experience for me. I had no idea that there were people who didn't want to control or berate me for things I wanted. It is a weird healing moment to realize that this was your normal for so long: that your thoughts, ideas, and dreams were not of value. This is where that grief comes in again. That is really sad! It is not hard to **ask** someone what they want or why they think the way they do. However, those who have treated us like we are below or subhuman will make us forget we had a sense of self at all! That is why figuring it out on this other side is so valuable for helping you design the life you want.

The benefit of learning more about ourselves is it helps us make decisions. We start to look at things like our career, how we like to decorate our own house, what type of person attracts us romantically, what we like to wear, emotional environments we want to be in, and more. The more data you collect about yourself, the easier it is to make decisions. This is a hallmark of any decision we need to make. If you are someone who struggles, or have struggled, to make decisions, then the best way to do that is to collect all the data you can about a topic. The more information we have, the easier it is to make a decision. I hear some of you naysayers go, "But that's not true! Have you ever been down the cereal aisle at the grocery store? There are so many choices. It is overwhelming!" Yeah, that is because you don't have your preferences sorted out. Do you have a particular flavor you like? Do you have issues with any specific ingredient? Have you noticed how you felt after you ate certain cereals? These questions make your decision way easier. It cuts a lot of options out and narrows it down by quite a bit! This works with almost any situation. The world does try to overwhelm us with decisions, but the more educated you are about your own beliefs and ideas, the easier they become.

Accepting love becomes scary at this stage, too. It is difficult to trust if a person actually means what they say. It takes a lot of time and adjustments to learn people's intentions toward us. No one wants to repeat old patterns. Luckily, with the grief work we can see areas that could be popping up again a bit easier than before. When we have any relationship that is better than what we are used to, it can become our new baseline. For example, if you only have had abusive romantic relationships, if your next relationship is not abusive that can be your new baseline. If that relationship ends and you find someone who is very nurturing that can be the higher baseline. You can see that your standards for what you are asking for can be raised up from what you are used to. Ideally, we are back to having the minimal baseline be that they treat you like a person. Which, to me, is sad because there are so many relationships where the basic baseline is not being a person. I hope we want to have thriving lives, not just, "Well, I am breathing, so I am okay" lives.

Grieving the good is realizing that there is so much good about who you are. There is so much genuine joy to feel in your day-to-day life. The qualities you possess, the way you make people feel, the gift you bring others by being yourself—may for the first time be seen by you. It is hard to believe people when they say good things about you, and your absorbability wasn't in the best place when you were in survival mode. Believing that you are loved, valued, and wanted is a scary thing to accept after being treated poorly. It takes some adjustments. It takes some time to remember the you you used to be or get to know the you you never met. You are worth the battle because you don't know where your future might bring you. You don't know who you will meet or where life takes you. You matter—because no one knows the future, and you may be the key to someone else's!

GRIEVING THE GOOD IS REALIZING THAT THERE IS SO MUCH GOOD ABOUT WHO YOU ARE. THERE IS SO MUCH GENUINE JOY TO FEEL IN YOUR DAY-TO-DAY LIFE.

CHAPTER NINE

BRAIN CHEMISTRY

I want to touch on only a few areas of the brain that get affected by abusive situations and consistent toxicity. We will look at these briefly, as there are many great books that discuss these brain structures in depth. I want to start by acknowledging that your brain is an organ that changes within your environment. It will literally shift the perspective you have on the world depending on your circumstances. In survival mode, your brain hyper-focuses on one perspective—in order to survive the threat. Survival mode causes you to miss all the other options available because your brain is not able to catalog other ideas, perceptions, or beliefs. You are unaware that this is an option because your brain won't let you prioritize it. Fear is the hardest wiring in the brain. When you are no longer just surviving, your brain might not know how to leave this state. That is how self-sabotaging happens. One way to help you not self-sabotage is to understand the structures of the brain. The more logic you can put into your understanding of yourself, i.e., data, the easier it is for you to see the importance of prioritizing your healing. I will only briefly touch on the right amygdala, the general area of the limbic system, the Broca, and the hippocampus. If you enjoy neuroanatomy, I strongly encourage you to read books that dive into it[5]. It is so amazing how our brain adapts to things! However, I am a nerd and very much enjoy reading about things—I don't expect that of everyone. That's

---

[5] See footnote 7

why I'm gonna try to explain, to the best of my ability, the importance of understanding why this matters so much and why emotional healing is a top priority.

Neuro-informed people tend to accept their humanness a bit better. When you understand the brain, you can better understand "the why." When we have a decent grasp of the why, we are able to accept our realities. What I mean by the why is the why's to all your questions: "Why do I act this way? Why do others act this way? Why am I like this? Why do I do that?" When you learned what a scab was for the first time, I'm sure you experienced some relief that it meant your skin would come back. I'm sure when you learned that the earth was round and that you were not going to fall off the edge, you were grateful.

NEURO-INFORMED PEOPLE TEND TO ACCEPT THEIR HUMANNESS A BIT BETTER. WHEN YOU UNDERSTAND THE BRAIN, YOU CAN BETTER UNDERSTAND "THE WHY."

Having a better understanding of your brain will not only give you grace for your mistakes, but it will remind you that your brain is an organ with its own healing process like any other organ in your body.

Let's start with our reptilian brain. The reptilian brain is in charge of basic survival bodily functions, i.e., eating, sleeping, crying, breathing, feeling temperature, hunger, pain, and going to the bathroom (van der Kolk, 2014). A lot of people have heard of the reptilian brain, however, you may not have considered how your stress symptoms relate to these functions. How have you been sleeping? How is your sex drive? Are you more or less hungry lately? Yup, those are all regulated by the reptilian brain and affected by stress.

When we are in a state of trauma, our right amygdala enlarges. This is because our brain naturally adapts to our environment. The amygdala is an almond shaped structure within the temporal lobes, and its job is to process emotions and memories. The main emotions it focuses on are the typical "negative" emotions, such as fear, anxiety, and aggression. It often is more simulated by threatening and dangerous behavior. The right amygdala is involved in social and emotional learning, often recognizing and interpreting facial expressions, body language, and other nonverbal cues that convey emotional information. The amygdala, including the right hemisphere, is closely connected with the formation and consolidation of emotional memories. It helps encode and store memories associated with emotionally significant events, which can influence future behavior and emotional responses. Our right amygdala's job is to assess danger and make sure that the danger shoots directly toward our limbic system. In its briefest sense, it stores emotions with other memories. Overall, the right amygdala plays a critical role in emotional processing, threat detection, and the regulation of emotional responses, contributing to our ability to navigate and adapt to our environment. This part of our brain gets affected in toxic relationships because it provides the signal to say, "Look, the scary thing is happening again!" The threat detection area gets more sensitive. Learning to help your brain see true threats, versus perceived threats, takes a lot of practice and cognitive awareness.

Right above the reptilian section of your brain is the limbic system. One of the functions of this area of the brain is to monitor survival threats. This is in charge of the fight/flight/freeze/fawn responses. Thanks to the research of Dr. Stephen Porges, what we can gather from the polyvagal theory is that our neuroception decides for us which of these four responses to pick. You don't electively pick which survival method would work best for you—your brain does that automatically. The reason for this is that the signal takes longer to pass through your thalamus to your prefrontal cortex than it does to directly go to your limbic system (Porge, 2011). A lot of times we blame ourselves for how our brain chose to survive something. I hope this helps you better understand why you reacted the way you did to a specific situation. Hopefully, you can forgive your brain for protecting you the best way it knew how.

Our limbic system, known as our reptilian brain, has many roles. Let's keep looking at the fight/flight/freeze/fawn responses. Its job is literally to keep you alive. It is not a structure as much as it is interconnected regions. Some of the regions are the hippocampus, right amygdala, thalamus, cingulate cortex, and mammillary bodies. These all work very hard to regulate your emotions and prioritize the life-threatening ones. I don't think people understand how important this is in context. A lot of people don't realize that their body purposefully shuts off other, non-threatening stimuli to focus on keeping you alive. Let us look an an example of this. Let's say you are in the woods and realize a bear is chasing you. Obviously, you run. As you are running, you are not thinking about anything besides getting out of the woods and away from the bear. You are stepping on things, branches are scraping you, you are on an adrenaline high, and, for a second, you turn around and see the bear is gone. You get this rush of release that the bear is out of sight. Then, right after your first big breath, you go *OUCH!* You realize that both arms are bleeding and all scraped up and you probably broke a toe. You didn't realize any of this while running. Only after you signaled safety to your brain did your mind bring your attention to the parts of you that need care. This is how the brain works. So many people think that once they are out of the survival stage, TA DA, we are done! Yeah, no. This is when you start to recognize all the other areas of your life that need healing. Some of those things that you haven't been paying attention to have been utterly detrimental in other areas, but you had no way of realizing it! Your brain catalogs these issues as "secondary" because they aren't life-threatening, they just hurt like a...beach.

When we are in our limbic system, our brain adapts and enlarges and shrinks in other areas. One of those areas is the Broca. This area shrinks while we are handling trauma. The Broca was named after a French physician named Paul Broca. Its main job is in the production of speech and language processing. It's got a circular looking shape to it (van der Kolk, 2014). One of my favorite things about the Broca is that it is considered a crucial development in human evolution. The reason this area is so cool is that its job is to take subjective material and translate it into logical phrases to express. Have you ever seen artwork and tried to articulate how it makes you feel? That's the Broca. The Broca's job also helps with emotions and translating them into communicative language for someone else to understand—so you can be understood. Why is this important? People who are in trauma have a smaller Broca (van der Kolk, 2014). It is exponentially more difficult to articulate what is happening to you. People feel scared and confused by you if you try to explain how you feel because you are not articulating it very well, and no one can relate. The Broca has potential to heal, but there isn't a lot of research on that yet. Starting to heal is necessary for communicating your experiences to others so understanding between people can happen.

The hippocampus, as stated earlier, is a part of the limbic system. However, it plays several functioning roles. It is crucial for memory formation and spatial navigation. Typically, this is where explicit memories take hold. When you think of a memory, do you often see it replay in your head like a mini movie? That's your hippocampus! Lots of neurolinguistic programming and hypnotherapy work in this region. Our hippocampus is also in charge of spatial awareness. Remember earlier when we were talking about our perception? Our sense of physical space in the world is changed in our hippocampus. How we see ourselves inside space and time and in relation to other objects are understood in the hippocampus. This is why the example of you running away from the bear is so important—you didn't take into account branches or other objects because they weren't a priority. Therefore, the hippocampus doesn't prioritize bumps, bruises, etc., because they are not life-threatening. How many emotionally damaging areas do you have that you just couldn't realize before? It is not possible to understand what you cannot understand. How do you understand things you can't yet? You heal!

Think again of the movie *Inside Out*. Remember the tube that Sadness and Joy went up into when they were in headquarters? (Docter & Carmen, 2015). That is a great representation of one of the jobs of the hippocampus. Imagine that one of those balls that needs to get processed and sent to long-term memory is too large to go through the tube. That is how symptoms work. The ball gets stuck, bounces out, and then tries to go through the tube again. When it isn't working, it creates symptoms. Those symptoms are measurable. That's why we have the Diagnostic Statistical Manual (DSM). Healing painful moments and memories mean taking that oversized ball and chopping it up so it can be processed and refiled into long-term memory and stop causing detrimental, self-sabotaging symptoms. How do we divide the large ball into bite sized pieces? The formula again: We cry, we grieve, we say goodbye, we sleep well (you should always sleep well after you give yourself a good cry—it's necessary to process neurotoxins and support the long-term memory filing system), we collect data about ourselves, we heal other sitting emotions, we communicate well with others, we hold ourselves accountable in all ways, and we constantly work on it. The more you know, the less ignorant you will be about your brain's function, role, and responsibilities, which is sometimes our most validating knowledge.

~~~~~~~~~~~~~~~~~~~

The beauty of our brain's capacity for healing is described with a fancy word: neuroplasticity. This allows our brain to make new associations with new experiences. This can be either a good or bad thing. Luckily, if we focus on the fact that we have the ability to change our neuron connections, we have a better chance of allowing the neurons we want to fire together to fire together and the ones we want to fire apart to fire apart.[6] You can decide if old memories can be attached to new experiences. It takes some practice, but it is doable. Overall, I hope you can see that your brain is here to get you to a place of learned growth.[7]

---

[6] Don't say that too fast: it sounds like fart. Saying out loud "fire a fart" is really embarrassing. I've done it too many times, so this is your warning for a potential occupational hazard.

---

[7] If you are more interested in this, I would strongly recommend these books: *The Body Keeps the Score* by Bessel van der Kolk, *The Brain That Changes Itself* by Norman Doidge, *The Polyvagal Theory* by Stephen W. Porges, and *Accessing the Healing Power of the Vagus Nerve* by Stanley Rosenberg. Just to name a few! This topic is fun for me, but these authors go into way more detail than the focus of this book allows.

The beauty of neuroplasticity is how I've watched it work inside of grief. I believe that when we grieve, the object of our grief is transported to a new part of our brain. I wonder if neuroplasticity is an instrumental part of that movement and has more activity in a grief state. I don't have hard evidence for this, but it is fascinating to see how people's language and view of a problem change after they let themselves take that big breath after a hard cry. It is an area for further exploration but there has to be a reason why the pain doesn't feel the same way after.

... IT IS FASCINATING TO SEE HOW PEOPLE'S LANGUAGE AND VIEW OF A PROBLEM CHANGE AFTER THEY LET THEMSELVES TAKE THAT BIG BREATH AFTER A HARD CRY.

Your brain is an organ. A lot of us who struggle with perfectionism really hate this reality. Like any other organ in your body, when your brain is hurt or struggling, it needs healing. It has its own process and its own way of dealing with the environment and relationships that we have day to day. It takes time, inconvenience, and intentional care to heal. If this were easy, everyone would do it. The reason you are reading this is probably because you care and want a different way of living than the one you are in right now. Typically, people who read self-help books are those who want to try to learn and be better. That is why knowing this information is so important. I hope you can see how this knowledge can be important to your healing and you have a better understanding of your responses and reactions. It has the ability to give yourself and others grace and I am optimistic that it has provided you some useful information to take with you as you continue this emotional journey.

CHAPTER TEN

ACCOUNTABILITY AND VULNERABILITY

I believe lack of accountability and responsibility is inexcusable. The reason you are healing in your journey right now is because other people refused to take accountability for how they destroyed your soul. You are in a position of knowing the damage this does to people around you. With apologies to Spiderman, with this knowledge comes great responsibility—thank you, Uncle Ben. It is your job to make emotional and mental healing a top priority. The most efficient avenue is to take accountability for what you have unintentionally done to others. Accountability requires vulnerability.

This is another area where I believe our society gives us a bald-faced lie. Vulnerability used well has the potential to be our greatest connector to others. I would classify vulnerability into two categories: claiming victimhood or owning your humanness, fostering deeper connections, and holding your power. I am talking about the latter. This type of vulnerability is necessary for accountability and boundaries. Let's use a marriage situation as an example because those are fun. If you are struggling with your in-laws, and you go up to your spouse and say, "Hey babe, I need to talk to you about this. I really care about your mom, and I think that is why when she is critical of me, it hurts my feelings a lot. I have a difficult time engaging with her because she always has something to say about how I decorate the house or how I handle the kids. I wish she would just think that I was a good enough wife for you and want to love me, too."

This allows for conversation. This vulnerable communication opens people up to want to hear what you have to say. That is a very hard statement to get mad about. You need to be comfortable in saying this about yourself and receiving this openness well from someone else. For perspective purposes, would you rather know all the stuff about someone that would make or break your relationship or wait for a massive blow up and a possible divorce? Choose your pain. Most people attempt this and then back out and make excuses like, "This isn't the right time." This is an avoidant tactic, and typically people who say this won't do it until they feel pushed to the very edge. Which, by the way, is just poor self-discipline. If you struggle with self-discipline, it means you also lack self-trust. In order to gain self-trust, you have to hit the seven BRAVING principles we talked about earlier that Brené Brown wrote. The main trust points that are remedied by self-discipline are obviously betraying your own boundaries, reliability of self, accountability of self, and integrity (Brown, 2014). When you are able to give yourself and others the accountability and integrity that is needed, you have a good starting formula for vulnerability.

It is your job to take hold of the problems that other people have put on your shoulders. If you try to be a victim—you will stay a victim. *Now you have a map to not be a victim.* No one else is inside your head and understands your emotions the way you do—you are the only one who is equipped to understand what you need and why you need what you need. Making other people play the guessing game with you is manipulative and unfair. That is why setting boundaries and holding yourself accountable is one of the greatest skills that come of being on the other side of grief.

Taking ahold of your healing and having the necessary account-ability and responsibility will lead to the most authentic and fulfilling life you could image. Nothing remains hidden, conversations flow effortlessly, and embracing someone fully, embracing yourself com-pletely, all lead to a profound connection beyond what you might have imagined! Living an authentic life is one of the best-earned skill sets to benefit from. You do not want to keep secrets from yourself or other people—it causes confusion and frustration—which leads to more grief. I say, "Pick your hard." Pick the hard you want to deal with.

I hate with all my might the phrase "ignorance is bliss." It is one of the biggest lies in our society. Ignorance is a necessary ingredient for unnecessary and sometimes brutal surprises. I am talking to those who say this phrase because they don't want to know about bad or useful things. If we are shocked by something our brain takes longer to process it. You can experience this in real time. When you feel completely surprised by something, most people have a delayed response. Their

TAKING AHOLD OF YOUR HEALING AND HAVING THE NECESSARY ACCOUNTABILITY AND RESPONSIBILITY WILL LEAD TO THE MOST AUTHENTIC AND FULFILLING LIFE YOU COULD IMAGINE.

brain has to catch up to what just happened. That brief pause is your brain trying to put the data somewhere because it wasn't expecting it, especially if it was outside of a normal day to day situation. Sometimes surprises are good, but your brain still takes a minute to catalog it that way. If you love good surprises, I'm not telling you to not like them. Please enjoy those if you do! If it is a bad surprise it has to put that information somewhere. Surprises cause our brain to pause. Why would you want to feel unprepared for a bad surprise? If you understood that your brain is trying to make a quick survival decision based on the surprise why would you want to elect ignorance? Not having some basic knowledge of the brain because "ignorance is bliss" is a gamble I wouldn't encourage someone to subscribe to.

The other lie I hate in society is, "It is easier this way." No, it is not. It is more familiar, but it is definitely not easier! Your definition of what is harder might be skewed. Whether we like it or not, we have two choices when it comes to emotional healing. *We either choose to heal or we don't.* Both options are hard. Both are very different life paths. It seems like a small sentiment now, but like a ship in the ocean whose helmsperson slightly turns the wheel, you will end up in a completely different location down the line. If "this is just too hard," are you electively choosing a harder route that leads a more miserable life because...you want to? Familiarity is getting equated with safety? Familiarity and safety can be dangerous together if it is not supposed by logic. That's acting like you may not be the brightest crayon in the crayon box if you want to believe that. Let's not choose to stay electively ignorant of something you need to know to have a better life. Let's not succumb to stupid-people logic. Choosing to have lack of emotional intelligence is elective stupidity, and I just won't put up with it—you shouldn't, either.

*SEE APPENDIX FOR A POTENTIAL SPIRITUAL ABUSE PITFALL FOR THIS SECTION.

PERSONAL INSIGHT INTO DOING THIS WORK MYSELF

~~~~~~

Who am I? Why bother listening to me? Great questions. I ascribe to the view that I am nobody particularly important. I am just someone who really understands the mind of the unhealthy. My backstory is interesting to people, I suppose. I'll briefly include it as it may help give you a grasp on why I understand these concepts so well.

I was not raised by the healthiest of adults. Violence, abuse, manipulation, confusion, lying, and stealing were normal parts of my childhood. I didn't know anything different. I thought everyone was like that. It was jarring for me to learn that other people were not raised the way my sister and I were. It took a long time for me to understand how someone else's understanding of the world worked. I never learned how to trust, feel safe, be enough, or be empowered. I had to learn what these new ideas were after my childhood. I ended up growing up very fast—I wouldn't say that I ever actually had a childhood—I had a time when I was smaller, perhaps. Growing up fast is all I've ever known. When you are raised around people with these types of characteristics, you learn exactly what not to do. I care very deeply about helping people to never feel the way I felt. If you want help healing, I want to make sure you feel educated, heard, emotionally understood, and respected while I can give some insight into your healing.

I have an extensive background with very violent and unhealthy individuals. I know how they think. I know the patterns to watch for, I know how they operate, and I understand their intentions. I know why they do what they do, and I do my best to help people understand that these types of unhealthy people do not live in the world you do. There are many books on how unhealthy people operate, and it is important to protect yourself from these people. My favorite author who writes about this is Shahida Arabi. I love her book *Becoming the Narcissist's Nightmare*. Her perspective on how to handle boundaries with the most soul crushing and aggressive people in our society is amazing. I like her writing because it is authentic, genuine, and blunt: all traits I very much appreciate.

The main focuses of the unhealthy people that surrounded me are power and control. These are the main motivators because they get people to do exactly what they want. The tactics toward me were mostly victimization, intellectual rhetoric, use of logical fallacies, lying, stealing, blaming, cheating, and betrayal, just to name a few. Each one of these tactics is purely to benefit the perpetrator—a paradigm also known as Machiavellian. They do not care if you are hurt, they just care that they get what they want from you. As long as you are useful, you are not discarded. I do love to burst people's bubbles because these people do actually exist. I love how people swear up and down that all other people think the way they think. There are people who do not think the way you think. They do not live in your world. People who believe all people are good have logic against them. Most everyone recognizes that there are good and bad people in the world. Who in the world do you think these "bad people" are? You think they are just out there on another planet? No. They are people, which means they have mothers, fathers, spouses, siblings, children, and friends. I think people who are willing to abuse others know intellectually that their victims won't believe that of them. A method these people commonly use is to take advantage of good people's worldview that abusive or manipulative people are well-intentioned. The victims give the abusers permission to hurt people longer by banking on the belief that the abuser thinks like the victim does. That's what makes these "good people" ignorant. They just can't believe someone would intentionally act the way they do. There becomes this fog of there is no way that they meant that! We try to rationalize our decision that the hurt is all about how we are inter-preting it and not because the actions are just plain hurtful. This keeps us ignorant to the possibility that people are actually like this. That's why unhealthy people are so successful. It is also why healthy people perseverate on these issues and try to talk to anyone they can who will listen to them. Which, of course, brings us back to the healing portion because if you can't explain it, you can sound like the one who is unwell. Why are people like this? Because we let them be. We let them by not having boundaries. We let them hurt us and our children and those around us because we don't force it to stop. Boundaries make people safer. They allow space for healing. It is your turn to live your life.

HEALTHY PEOPLE QUESTION THEIR INTENTIONS AND CARE ABOUT SELF-REFLECTION. UNHEALTHY PEOPLE DON'T. THAT'S AN EASY MEASURE TO GO AGAINST.

If you are wondering if you are one of these people, it is very likely that you are not. Healthy people question their intentions and care about self-reflection. Unhealthy people don't. That's an easy measure to go against. Good mothers worry about not being good mothers, etc. Now, a lot of people argue for redemption. I am not God, and it is not my job to tell you who to forgive or who not to forgive. How you let other people treat you is purely on you. Take what is useful, discard what is not useful, and apply the principles that make the most sense to you. Allow yourself to ask, and eventually demand, that you be treated like a person and not talked to or used like you are an object. It takes practice and—you guessed it—grief.

From personal experience of doing the grief work myself—this is the best I have ever felt. I am the most physically healthy I have ever been (thanks to getting rid of years of constant cortisol), I am the most mentally attuned I have ever been, and I feel very confident in the person I am today—even though I have been given every reason not to feel that way. I hold healthy relationships, I love the family I created, and I love my children with all my heart. I don't pass my grief down to them. I am learning new things about myself all the time, and I love it! Thriving instead of surviving is one of the most amazing gifts of going through this process. My articulation of how the brain works seems to land well with people, the way I hold people's hands through this process seems to have some effects on people, and my constant reading and research from being a nerd has benefited me. I hope you were able to get a glimpse of some of that though this journey with me.

Freedom is worth the price. The emotional warfare of tears and saying goodbye to pieces of your soul is worth every regrowth. My past doesn't haunt me anymore, and I am forever grateful. There really is a far side to the grief. There comes a time when it doesn't sting the way the pain originally did. Waves of grief still form—but they do not stop me from healing. The point is not that the grief is all done, it is that you know how to grieve when it comes up. It is a skill that has to be used sadly more than not. Once you understand how to grieve well, the benefits always outweigh the pain. I hope you go forward knowing that the pain does not have to debilitate you—it can heal you. You are not alone. You matter. You are worth fighting for. Don't be afraid.

CONCLUSION

Grief is not a favorable topic because it hurts. Setting boundaries and relationship standards is difficult to do when you struggle with people pleasing. We do not have to live a life riddled with bitterness, hidden emotions, pain, and self-worth issues. Further, "Being emotionally mature—that is, having stable moods, being free of chronic anxiety and depression, controlling emotional outbursts—isn't possible if one is hiding from the past" (*Black*, 2004, p. 128). Growing in our own emotional maturity and resiliency is a difficult feat, but the benefits are powerful. Our relationships might have encouraged us to believe that we are not worthy of being seen as a human. We may have few examples, if any, to show that we are worth being spoken to, treated as, and appreciated as humans. We have different levels of closeness in our lives, and it is important to keep those boundaries and regulate our emotions.

Whether we are dealing with a significant other, parent, child, or authority figure, we need to set boundaries when they have made decisions about who we are. We have to accept that the people around us have a story about us in their heads. Whatever that story may be, we know that it is up to them to change. We cannot make any person do anything. We cannot make someone love us. We cannot wish that they see us as valuable. We can only honor and respect what they have chosen. This allows us the freedom we need to be as close or as far away as we need, physically and emotionally.

Grief is painful. Emotional resiliency takes time. Grief is a skill. It is hard to undo what society has taught us about how sadness works. Sadness is designed to be a healing agent—not a pity party. Moving into grief and healing yourself will never make you a victim to other people's decisions about you. Your brain's job is to help file data into the appropriate area of your brain. Your brain and emotions all work together to protect you and heal the areas you cannot get back. Grief means stepping into the pain—allowing it to hurt the way it needs to hurt. Grief doesn't feel good—but no pain will. All pain is annoying, inconvenient, hurtful, and frustrating. That is how it is designed. Our body knows how to heal wounds and can heal emotional ones, too—we just have to give the brain permission to let it hurt. Don't let yourself forget the feeling you get after a good, heavy, long cry. You take a deep breath, and things feel different. That difference will help your perspective and allow your mood to shift differently as well. Grief needs to happen in a safe space. It is important that you cry with those you trust or do it alone. Saying goodbye to living people is not what we elected to do. It requires respecting that there are parts of us, or all of us, that they do not want.

I hope that as you journey through your pain, you realize how important, resilient, and needed you are in the world. People can try to take your dignity and destroy your soul, but you can decide to not let them. You can give yourself power back by healing. No one gets to write your story but you. You can have the life you wanted to design for yourself—don't let yourself get in your own way because grieving is hard. Just because it hurts doesn't mean it's bad. You are worth every ounce of healing. You don't know what your future holds, so you don't know that eventually you could be someone's whole world. Don't think that our emotions don't catch up to us—they do. We either decide to heal or not to heal.

Initial pain of grief doesn't last forever. As life goes on, there are different layers we will need to grieve. It is not a one and done deal. Oftentimes, it comes in waves, and we have to let them hit as they surface. You will notice a shift in your grief after you become a puddle on the floor—sometimes several times. There is a far side. There is a sense of freedom that comes from being able to accept only the people who want to love you and show up for you in your life. You are allowed to have different measures of how you wish to be treated. It is up to those around you to decide whether that is reasonable or not. To be a healthy communicator, to say what you mean and mean what you say, is a sign your brain is healing. We all have our journeys, and it is our responsibility to not hurt the people around us because we are hurt. We must stop the pattern—and remember to love ourselves and others well.

APPENDIX
POTENTIAL SPIRITUAL ABUSE PITFALLS

IMPORTANCE OF STICKING TO BOUNDARIES: "WHY ARE YOU STILL UPSET ABOUT THIS?"

We cannot deny that God made boundaries with Jesus. We have to know this and know where to find it. I think our very best example of the grief in boundaries is Hebrews 5:7–10, "During the days of Jesus' life on earth, he offered up prayers and petitions with fervent cries and tears to the one who could save him from death, and he was heard because of his reverent submission. Son though he was, he learned obedience from what he suffered and, once made perfect, he became the source of eternal salvation for all who obey him and was designated by God to be high priest in the order of Melchizedek" (*Zondervan NIV Study Bible*, 1985/1995/2002).

I really want to highlight how incredible this is. Jesus *knew* He had to die and pleaded with God and asked Him to not let this happen to Him. Jesus at this point did not want to die! He was crying, realizing what it meant to lose His life. The boundary God set was **no**. It is heartbreaking to know you desperately don't want to deal with something and even *God* won't save you. That is amazingly painful, and even Jesus cried. Are you above Jesus? I hope not. You have to go through pain and grief and loss, too—you are not immune to it in any way. He is a perfect model of healthy emotion. You never see Jesus say, "Oh, well, crying is bad!" That is human ridiculousness. God literally made boundaries with Jesus. Jesus cried about it because it was so devastating. When boundaries are made—grief can follow.

What happened when God set that boundary? Jesus became **our literal savior**. Jesus honored God's boundary, and He became the most important person in our relationship to God. Honoring boundaries is good for everyone, even when there is no way you could see that from your present perspective.

On the other side of the coin is relief, as we see biblically that Jesus rises from the dead. I am sure His friends were surprised and relieved! It is very common that once you make a boundary and move through the grief, you will find relief. Most will notice that you do not have your energy sucked dry, and people treat you differently. I often hear people say they can't imagine their lives without boundaries once they learn how to set them because they feel free. It is worth giving yourself the chance to feel some freedom and relief! That is the gift of this hard work and pain. Fruits of your labor, if you will. Give it a shot, and if I'm wrong, then burn the book and never try to heal this way again, but still do try to heal.

It is also why we cannot spiritually abuse people to shame them out of crying. You or they are not above Jesus, so to say to them that they "need to get over it" is a spiritually abusive statement. To call someone "weak" or a "wussy" for meaningful loss is destructive. Would you talk to Jesus like that if he were crying? I hope not.

It is okay to tell people "This isn't the time to cry, let's wait till we are in a safer place." It is not okay to ridicule them for having a sad emotion. These are valid emotions and we need to encourage them with people not shame them. Our job is to show up for people and be vulnerable with them in their sadness and acknowledge that their emotions are exactly right. We need to reflect the emotions we hear and sit with them in their devastation. Let them talk and assure them that their emotions are valid.

ROMANTIC RELATIONSHIPS: "GOD DOESN'T GIVE YOU MORE THAN YOU CAN HANDLE!"

We are allowed to make boundaries in our marriage and intimate relationships. When you make a commitment to someone and promise to stick to your vows, then you break them, you completely uproot your significant other's life. If there are kids involved, their whole lives change, too, as does the way they view relationships. You can either decide to stay with someone who broke your boundaries or make sure it never happens again. Depending on the breakage it is important to know what your last straw issues are. When a major boundary betrayal happens and leads to divorce or break up, it is so intense because there is a wedding album, events, promises in front of everyone, children, and a home and bed. There is a reason that God set up marriage the way He did. It is a covenant that *can* be broken. There is a reason that God does not allow himself to be abused by His people over and over again in the Old Testament. He breaks the covenant because they broke it first. He provides the natural boundary and consequences for abusing him. God really is an amazing example of healthy boundaries—it is all over the Old and New Testaments.

One easy example is the story of the Golden Calf. Here is what He says about being betrayed by His people by worshiping a golden cow: "I have seen these people," the Lord said to Moses, "and they are a stiff-necked people. Now leave me alone so that my anger may burn against them and that I may destroy them. Then I will make you into a great nation" (*Zondervan NIV Study Bible*, 1985/1995/2002, Exodus 32:9–10). We can see how angry God is here. Let's not get stuck on what is considered "bad emotions." God *is* angry in this example. Therefore, to detest healthy emotions such as anger, sadness, and pain are not what is asked of us. Anger is allowed, it is about how you handle your anger. Of course I am not saying you have permission to destroy people but you are allowed to say enough is enough. Anger in this situation comes from pain. When other people do not value the relationship as much as we do sadness and anger are apart of that goodbye process.

When people are struggling in their romantic relationships it is not our job to tell them God is not giving them more than they can handle. That is dismissive. God absolutely gives us more than we can handle. That is a poor misquote of 1 Corinthians 12-13: "So, if you think you are standing firm, be careful that you don't fall! No temptation has seized you except what is common to man. And God is faithful; he will not let you be tempted beyond what you can bear. But when you are tempted, he will also provide a way out so that you can stand up under it" (*Zondervan NIV Study Bible*, 1985/1995/2002). Emotional overwhelm means we are dealing with more than we can handle. What we need to say in this situation is something along the lines of "This is all too much right now and it is supposed to be," or "You let yourself feel everything you need to feel" or "It is okay to not be okay for awhile." If you are looking for something healing those are often much better phrases to say.

PARENTS:
"BUT HONOR THY MOTHER AND FATHER!"

If you have heard this phrase thrown at you in a spiritually abusive way, it's because it *actually was* a spiritually abusive statement made toward you. The most famous quote is Ephesians 6:1–3. My *favorite* part about this is that when people use it for abusive purposes, they never quote verse four. Literally, verse four is, "Fathers, do not exasperate your children; instead, bring them up in the training and instruction of the Lord" (*Zondervan NIV Study Bible*, 1985/ 1995/2002). A father is asked to not force their kids to feel like their standards are too high and impossible to meet. If at any point, a child tells their dad that they feel this way, the Bible demands that the dad " . . . bring them up in the training and instruction of the Lord." This is an expression of emotional protection for children. It is designed for children to feel mentally and emotionally safe. Let's look at this verse a bit further.

"'Honor your father and mother'—which is the first command-ment with a promise . . . " (*Zondervan NIV Study Bible*, 1985/1995/ 2002, Ephesians 6:2). I love this verse. Why? Because it provides children who have been abused with spiritual protection for making boundaries. You might ask, "What? What do you mean? How so?" Well, let's start with these questions: Whose definition of honor do you think this is? Is it *your* definition of honor? Is it your *parents'* definition of honor? Or is it *God's* definition of honor? Think on that. Whose definition of the word "honor" have you been living by? Society's? Yikes. Honor means respect. Respect means boundaries because boundaries mean love. This verse protects the most vulnerable from abuse. Let me give you an example: Your mother or father had a pattern of humiliating you in front of friends and neighbors. They did it to you your whole life. They talked about your most embarrassing moments and why you were not on honor-roll and critiqued you every chance they could. Let's say you are 24 years old now, and you tell them, "If you guys say something else humiliating about me to my new girlfriend when I bring her over, I will not visit for holidays anymore going forward—I am serious." Let's say, they don't listen to you. This is a theme, and they repeated the behavior. Also, in this scenario as so often is the case in life, I'm sure you've addressed it numerous times before, but this is the first time you actually mean it. Okay, so, they say a ton of embarrassing things about you in front of your new girlfriend. This time you were serious. You don't talk to or see your parents for three months. You get massive texts asking where you are, why don't you just get over it, saying you're too sensitive or you're acting immature, blah blah blah. You have had enough, and you respond like this:

"I have asked you my entire life to stop humiliating me for your own benefit in front of friends and family. I have felt so hurt and belittled by you, yet you seem to think that this is somehow okay. I will from now on continue to respect the fact that you do not see me as a son worth being proud of. I will honor your beliefs about who I am in your eyes. I will honor that you have decided that I am nothing more than an embarrassment to have as a son. I will respect your decision to no longer be an embarrassment to you and not show up in front of friends or family. You have made your feelings about me clear for 24 years, and I think I am finally at a point where I can believe you. I will honor your views of me. Please do not contact me going forward, as you have made your view of me very clear."

Welcome to understanding what honor your mother and father actually mean! That was of course a more drastic consequence for the parents. Or, obviously on a lighter note, to just never bring anyone over to the house! The point is that it means believing them when they make clear who they believe you to be. Once parents, or people in general, have made a decision about us, it is our job to **honor** that decision. To **respect** that choice. That is your job when it comes to honoring your mother and father. It is your job to respect the choices they have already made about you. If that means they don't love you, you sadly have to respect that decision. You are not God, so you cannot change their minds and make them love you. You have to honor them the way they have made it clear they should be honored. Of course, at this point I hope you have tried other avenues such as conflict resolution to try and resolve disagreements. However, there can come a point where what they feel and believe about you is just what it is. That's when a boundary might be needed.

This also means we cannot shame any adult child about a boundary they made with a parent. Instead of accusing the adult child of why they may have a strained relationship with their parent, we might want to **not** insert our own opinions about that to an adult child. All because we are friends with their parent does not make it our place to step in. People don't typically make the hard choice not to have a relationship with their parents lightly. Often the adult child has fought tooth and nail for the relationship with no avail. We need to respect decisions when adult children or parents make boundaries. It is not okay for us to try and step in and assume we know best by saying something like "honor thy mother and father."

CHILDREN: "SPARE THE ROD"

"Whoever spares the rod hates their children, but the one who loves their children is careful to discipline them (*Zondervan NIV Study Bible*, 1985/1995/2002, Proverbs 13:24). Weird! It is almost like the Bible tells us as parents to *make boundaries*. Wild theology that is. I do appreciate this version of the Bible because King James has it out that discipline means to hit your kids. Disciplining and hitting your children are different things. I do not encourage hitting children. The messaging in that is damaging. Small children haven't developed enough to understand why they are getting physically hurt for something. It also teaches them that if someone else does something wrong, they can hit the other person. Why can't they? Children should not be physically hurt by an adult who they have no way of defending against. They need support expressing their emotions and regulating well. I'll just say if you are someone who spanks your kids or believes that is okay, this section isn't for you because I can't condone that. Safety is vital to properly establish boundaries and discipline. This helps all children develop, regardless of their age.

When a parent is not disciplining their child over something you think they should be there are better ways to broach this topic than to say "spare the rod." Back to the point I make in the preface, if someone *asks* for our opinion or help, that is different than throwing our own opinion in their face. Disciplining children at different stages of development is hard! There are a lot of intricacies with it because we want to make sure that children understand what they did, but not do in a way that is outside of their developmental stage. With every kid being unique, they all respond differently to different stimuli! It is a hard balance to keep and there isn't an overall right answer. I think that is on purpose because disciplining happens inside of a safe relationship. The measure of a safe relationship is in the eyes of those, well, in the relationship.

ACCOUNTABILITY AND VULNERABILITY: "IGNORANCE IS BLISS"

This is a scary platitude to live by or say out loud for others to live by. Ignorance means that we are allowing knowledge not to be important to us and deciding that not learning something is too hard. Ignorance has a way of just leaving problems till later. I do not believe God asks us to stay stupid. That feels a bit counterproductive to having a relationship with God. If you are someone who uses this mantra for themselves I would gently ask you to reconsider. Depending on how this phrase is used, even towards yourself, can come off dismissive. I encourage people to learn more about themselves and others. If we can try to understand God's creation, we have a better understanding of God. We have a duty to understand perspectives different than ours. Not always needing to agree, but to understand. The phrase that "hurt people hurt people" is true. That is a **choice**. Once you have acknowledged unhealed parts of yourself, it is important to start working on it and not choosing to stay ignorant.

When someone shares a major event with you that they feel is important, it is dismissive to respond with, "I don't need to know; ignorance is bliss." Someone is trying to share something vulnerable with you and you shut them down. If you don't want to hear something, or even educate yourself on something, better phrases might be, "I understand this is really important to you and I am not able to receive this message well. I want you to feel good about who you tell this too," or "I am unable to hear this the way I think you want me too. I am sorry I am not the right person for this topic," or "I understand this means a lot to you and I love that you love it but I cannot enjoy this with you as much as I want too." These examples can be a more nurturing way to shut down a conversation than simply encouraging people to remain ignorant.

REFERENCES

Arabi, S. (2016). *Becoming the narcissist's nightmare: How to devalue and discard the narcissist while supplying yourself.* SCW Archer Publishing.

Black, K. (2001). *Mothering without a map.* Penguin Group.

Brickman, P., & Campbell, D. T. (1971). Hedonic relativism and planning the good society. In M. H. Apple (Ed.), *Adaptation-level theory* (pp. 287–305). New York: Academic Press.

Brown, B. (2015). *Rising Strong: The reckoning. The rumble. The revolution.* Spiegel & Grau.

Brown, B. (2021). *Atlas of the heart: Mapping meaningful connection and the language of human experience.* Penguin Random House.

Cloud, H. & Townsend, J. (1992). *Boundaries: When to say yes when to say no to take control of your life.* Zondervan Publishing House.

Devine, M. (2017). *It's OK that you're not OK: Meeting grief and loss in a culture that doesn't understand.* Sounds True.

Diener, E., Lucas, R. E., & Scollon, C. N. (2006). Beyond the hedonic treadmill: Revising the adaptation theory of well-being. *American Psychologist, 61*(4), 305–314. https://doi.org/10.1037/0003-066X.61.4.305

Docter, P. (Director), & Del Carmen, R. (Producer). (2015). *Inside out.* Pixar Animation Studios.

Doidge, N. (2008). *The brain that changes itself: Stories of personal triumph from the frontiers of brain science.* Penguin Books.

Edelman, H. (2006). *Motherless mothers: How losing a mother shapes the parent you become.* Harper.

FutureLearn. (n.d.). *Trauma, neuro, and shame awareness: Understanding trauma.* FutureLearn. https://www.futurelearn.com/info/courses/trauma-neuro-and-shame-awareness/0/steps/392676#:~:text=Coined%20by%20Dr.,risk%2C%20even%20before%20conscious%20awareness

Gibson, L. C. (2015). *Adult children of emotionally immature parents: How to heal from distant, rejecting, or self-involved parents.* New Harbinger Publications.

Goleman, D. (1994). *Emotional intelligence: The groundbreaking book that redefines what it means to be smart.* Random House.

Hebb D. 1949. *The organisation of behaviour.* New York, NY: John Wiley and Sons.

Kübler-Ross, E., & Kessler D. (2005). *On grief & grieving: Finding the meaning of grief through the five stages of loss.* Scribner.

O'Conner, M. F. (2022). *The grieving brain: The surprising science of how we learn from love and loss.* Harper Collins.

Porges, S. W. (2011). *The polyvagal theory: Neurophysiological foundation of emotions, attachment, communication, and self-regulation.* W. W. Norton & Company.

Rosenberg, S. (2017). *Accessing the healing power of the vagus nerve: Self-help exercises for anxiety, depression, trauma, and autism.* North Atlantic Books.

Rowling, J. K. (2000). *Harry Potter and the Goblet of Fire.* Scholastic.

Scaer, R. (2012). *8 keys to brain–body balance.* W. W. Norton & Company.

van der Kolk, B. (2014). *The body keeps the score: Brain, mind, and body in the healing of trauma.* Penguin Books.

Walker, P. (n.d.). *The four F's trauma typology: Fight, flight, freeze, and fawn.* Retrieved August 25, 2024, from https://pete-walker.com/fourFs_TraumaTypologyComplexPTSD.htm

Young, W. P. (2008). *The shack: where tragedy confronts eternity.* Windblown Media.

Zondervan NIV Study Bible. (1985/1995/2002). Zondervan.

ABOUT THE AUTHOR

Laura Moulton is a psychotherapist and the owner of her practice, where she currently enjoys clinical supervision work with new therapists. Laura is passionate about trauma, grief, and boundary-related issues. Laura earned her bachelor's degree in Sociology from the University of Colorado-Denver and her Master's degree in Counseling from Denver Seminary. She currently resides in Colorado with her husband and three daughters, where she enjoys reading, writing, and people-watching.

Credentials at the time of publication:
MA - Master of Arts in Counseling
LPC - Licensed Professional Counselor
NCC - National Certified Counselor
CIMHP - Certified Integrated Mental Health Professional
CCTP-II - Certified Clinical Trauma Professional, Level 2
CAGCS - Certified Advanced Grief Counseling Specialist
ACS - Approved Clinical Supervisor

Specialty Training:
EMDR - trained levels 1&2
Brainspotting - trained levels 1&2